Chess and the Art of Negotiation

Ancient Rules for Modern Combat

Anatoly Karpov and Jean-François Phelizon
with Bachar Kouatly

PRAEGER

Westport, Connecticut
London

Library of Congress Cataloging-in-Publication Data

Karpov, Anatoly, 1951-
    Chess and the art of negotiation : ancient rules for modern combat / Anatoly Karpov
    and Jean-François Phelizon with Bachar Kouatly.
      p. cm.
    Includes bibliographical references and index.
    ISBN 0–275–99065–6 (alk. paper)
    1. Chess.   I. Phélizon, Jean François.   II. Kouatly, Bachar.   III. Title.
GV1449.5.K35   2006
  794.1—dc22   2006020994

British Library Cataloguing in Publication Data is available

Library of Congress Catalog Card Number: 2006020994
ISBN: 0–275–99065–6

First published in 2006

This is a translation of the original French edition, published as:
Psychologie de la Bataille
©Ed. Economica, 2004

This book also has been translated into chinese as *Due Yi* © Citic, 2005

Praeger Publishers, 88 Post Road West, Westport, CT 06881
An imprint of Greenwood Publishing Group, Inc.
www.praeger.com

Printed in the United States of America

The paper used in this book complies with the
Permanent Paper Standard issued by the National
Information Standards Organization (Z39.48–1984).

10 9 8 7 6 5 4 3 2 1

Contents

Acknowledgments

We would like to extend our special thanks to Nicholas Philipson, our editor, for his complete support of this project, and for his constant encouragement, advice, and guidance. Our deepest appreciation also goes to Elva Lègére Clements and Dorothy Wackerman for their editorial comments, and to Christine Hammond for her help with whatever needed to be done.

Introduction

In this book, two masters in their respective areas of expertise—
Anatoly Karpov, former World Champion and grand chess master,
and Jean-François Phelizon, CEO of Saint-Gobain Corporation—
come together to share their insight into how the ancient game
of chess can be a blueprint for success in today's business world.

Ever since the game was believed to have been played for
the first time in sixth-century India, chess has been an intellectual
duel employing strategy, tactics, and psychology. Many of the lessons
learned by students of the game can be applied to a variety of business
management scenarios, especially negotiation.

Chess and the Art of Negotiation takes the form of a fascinating
dialogue between Mr. Karpov and Mr. Phelizon, moderated by Bachar
Kouatly, himself an international chess master. In this give-and-take
approach, the reader can get a better insight into the experiences
and thought processes of these experts as they convey both chess and
business theory and real-world applications.

Chess offers executives timeless lessons in a take-charge business approach that is aimed at winning. In business, negotiations can
reach the intensity of war, hence the reference to "combat" in the
subtitle. Analogies can be made on many levels, with opposing sides
being called "adversaries" or "opponents," and approaches being re-
ferred to in military terms such as "frontal," "oblique," and "lateral."

Mr. Phelizon makes numerous references throughout the dialogue about the strategies of the great Chinese general Sun Tzu, author of *The Art of War*, a book studied by nearly every military strategist. While every parallel *cannot* be drawn among chess, business, and combat—the fact that each side starts at an equal advantage on the chessboard and not in business and battle, for example—many of the same principles can be applied to each endeavor.

What sets *Chess and the Art of Negotiation* apart from other business management books is found in its focus on psychology. Both chess and business negotiation rely heavily on understanding the psychology of the opponent as one of the most important keys to success. Considering the psychological profile of the opponent and capitalizing on his or her strengths and weaknesses—and understanding and dealing with one's own strengths and weaknesses—will usually be what distinguishes a successful person in chess, business, or battle.

The style of a business executive or chess player can differ widely. There is the confrontational (getting something without giving in exchange) and the concessionary (being ready to offer something in exchange for what is wanted) styles. Approaches, as mentioned above, can range from direct or frontal (taking no account of the other's needs) to indirect or oblique (using the strengths and weaknesses of the other to one's advantage) to lateral (making the opponent negotiate before he even fights). Knowing what style and approach will work best for each individual situation is essential, such as working toward a long-term alliance rather than a negotiation with a single, one-time objective.

By reading *Chess and the Art of Negotiation*, the reader will find out

- Why it is always better to negotiate after your opponent has eaten but you've barely touched your meal
- Why it is best to negotiate in your own time zone
- Why humility can win out over ego
- Why you should never go into a fight alone
- How adverse advisors can break a logjam in negotiations
- How to seal the deal before the first word is exchanged
- How La Fontaine's Fables are invaluable tools to grasping an opponent's psychological profile

By implementing the wisdom found in *Chess and the Art of Negotiation*, what will the reader gain? Progressing through the topics of preparation for the battle, choosing the style and approach of the engagement, and participating in the actual negotiations, and the aftermath, the reader will be the silent listener to the conversation, the one who will gain a unique insight into the strategy and tactics of two men at the top of their game.

Establish and Maintain a Winning Position

Anatoly Karpov's story. – Jean-François
Phelizon's career and interests. – Finding
common ground. – Uncertainty in
negotiations and chess. – Putting "battle
logic" into place.

What greater victory can there be than convincing your enemy he cannot win?
Michel de Montaigne

Kouatly – In what way is a chess match like a negotiation? In what way is a negotiation like a chess match? In either case, what are the possible approaches? And finally, how is the psychological dimension inherent in all confrontations taken into account? The following five informative conversations, led by Anatoly Karpov and Jean-François Phelizon, try to answer these questions in many ways. First because they have stories, experiences, and personalities that are very different; second because they agree on the conclusions that are the basis for all tactical action; and finally because they both seem to favor finesse over force.

Anatoly, your personal story almost reads like a novel.

Karpov – Yes, I started playing chess very young, when I was just a little boy. First with my father, then with my friends, who often were four or five years older than I. In the beginning, naturally, I was far from thinking about a world championship title, but I loved chess and I could play day and night, hours and hours on end.

I think the first book I owned was about chess. I was eight years old and it was a book written by the great Cuban player Capablanca.[1] I was already a second-level player, almost first level. It probably seems strange today, but in 1959 it was extremely difficult to get books in Zlatoust, the town where I lived, especially books about chess.

Kouatly – That was the time of Gosplan[2] . . .

Karpov – Yes, it was still Gosplan. In order to find books on chess, you had to go to Chelyabinsk, the capital of Southern Oural province. But bookstores only received a few at a time and they were always out of stock, because there were so many chess amateurs.

At nine, I was already the best player in Zlatoust. I was sent to the Botvinnik[3] School. Of the seven students who were enrolled at this school, some of whom were older, I was without argument the one with the most determination and energy. I would often play all night until 7:00 in the morning and still get to the first class at 10:00 AM, bright-eyed and rested.

The first time I traveled abroad was in 1966 and I was fifteen. I had the opportunity to participate in a match in Sweden and we traveled in a group. The same year I also went to Groningen in Holland but this time alone. I could barely speak English and it was quite an adventure.

Back then, you couldn't just leave the country. You needed an authorization from the Sports Ministry and the Protocol Department. I had been given a passport with a visa and some travelers' checks drawn on a Russian bank. But no one in Holland wanted them and it was merely by coincidence that I found the only Dutch bank willing to cash them. I got on the Moscow-to-London train, which made a stop at Amersfoort, where I was supposed to change trains. But what train should I take? Groningen wasn't posted anywhere. I was all alone on the platform, hopeless and lost. Finally, someone put me on a train and told me to "change in Zwolle." I still remember it. And there again I was completely lost. Finally, I managed to arrive at my destination.

Kouatly – How were you able to secure championship matches?

Karpov – Well, it wasn't easy. At that time, there were many great chess players in the U.S.S.R. and not a lot of room for new talent. Coming from deep Russia, I had no backing. I had to start by becoming an international master.

In 1968, I entered the University of Moscow, and in 1969 I won my first tournament. That same year, I qualified for the World Junior Chess Championship, where I came in first. I remember that my trainer, someone with good sense, said to me, "Anatoly, because you play very well, you have become an international master, but there is still more road to travel before becoming a grand master. You can get there, but you must go step by step." He then got me interviews with people at the Ministry of Sports.

Kouatly – Maybe you should specify that in the U.S.S.R., chess has always been considered a sport.

Karpov – Yes, it is considered a sport just like swimming, gymnastics, or weight lifting. One day in August 1969, I asked to participate in a tournament organized by IBM that was to be held in Amsterdam in July 1970. A few weeks later, I was seen by the Sports Minister. He was holding a little notebook that he briefly consulted and then said to me, "No one is yet signed up for this tournament, so we can put your name down." I was ecstatic.

Unfortunately, in the spring of 1970 I received a phone call from one of the minister's people telling me that "Spassky[4] will be playing in Amsterdam and you will not be part of his team."

At the same time, Venezuela sent me an invitation to a tournament that hadn't been planned in the budget. So the first response from the Ministry of Sports was that no one from the U.S.S.R. would participate. But [Alexei] Kosygin had signed an agreement with Venezuela promoting cooperation in the areas of sports and culture. At that time I was living in Leningrad, a city from which it was very difficult to obtain travel authorization out of the U.S.S.R. The first time I requested permission to go to Venezuela, the Commission replied that they didn't know who I was and that I would need to stay at least a year in Leningrad before they would consider my application.

In Moscow, the Ministry of Sports had approved my request and had even obtained a visa for me. But the Leningrad Commission still had to give the green light for my travel, which it categorically refused to do.

Everything was at a standstill. The whole affair, as I learned later, went all the way up to Kosygin, who called the minister and said, "What is going on at your ministry? We just signed an agreement with Venezuela and they're telling me that the U.S.S.R. won't send any representatives to a tournament that they're organizing?" The minister answered, "Leningrad is creating the road block. The Commission doesn't want to give Karpov his exit authorization." So

Kosygin simply said, "Forget Leningrad and send Karpov," and I got my authorization the very next morning!

Kouatly – And that's how your international career started.

Karpov – It was in Caracas that I became an international grand master. I was the youngest ever. From then on in Russia I was considered a rising star. In any case, I never had any trouble after that participating in tournaments abroad. In 1971, I won two important tournaments, Moscow and Hastings, and continued to progress up the classification ranks. After that, I played against Polugaevsky, Spassky, and Korchnoi.[5]

Finally I became the second-ranked player in the world on February 28, 1973, and world champion on April 3, 1975, after Fischer refused to defend his title. Naturally, as world champion my life completely changed, because in the U.S.S.R. the authorities have always considered chess as one of the most prestigious sports.

Kouatly – Jean-François, you're not a chess master, but you do have much experience in the business world. You've also led many theoretical discussions on strategy.

Phelizon – Compared to Anatoly, my story is much less involved. On a personal level I lived many years in foreign countries. I spent most of my childhood in South America and I've also lived in Tunisia, Spain, and the United States, where I currently reside. My academic training is both in economics and science.

For years I was fascinated by information technology. I bought my first computer at the end of the 1970s before the advent of microtechnology. It was an old PDP8 that the computer department of an automobile manufacturer had sold me by weight instead of throwing it away. My family still remembers this monument that towered in the foyer and on which my children practiced their biorhythms. It consumed huge amounts of electricity and it couldn't be used at the same time as other home appliances. Should I admit that the correct resolution of research algorithms took priority? Thirty years later, I'm still not sure my family has forgiven me for all the interrupted clothes washings!

On a professional level, as the CFO and then Senior Vice President of one of the major French industrial groups, I've been fortunate to conduct important negotiations dealing mainly with divestitures or acquisitions. So, I have lived through those special times in a manager's life when surrounded by his team and trying to reach a certain goal. In some cases, it is a goal that could involve billions of euros. In those situations, you must reach agreement on dozens and dozens of items that are part of the transaction, and obviously you need to mobilize all your intellectual and tactical resources.

Finally, and this is almost another life, I am the author of a few books dealing with strategy—that is to say, strategy in general. As such, I've studied in depth the great theoreticians of strategic and tactical action, from Sun Tzu to Von Clausewitz and from Foch to Liddell Hart.[6] What impressed me most is without a doubt Sun Tzu, the great Chinese general who lived during the troubled time of the *Springs and Autumns*.[7] I've reread his little book *The Art of War* over and over—and even published an annotated translation. I'm also fond of another Chinese text, the *Thirty Six Stratagems*, which is less well known than Sun Tzu's but throws light in a very special way on the ins and outs of tactical action. In reality, *The Art of War* is to *Thirty Six Stratagems* what strategy is to tactics.

Kouatly – One evening, about a year ago, the three of us met at Jean Pavlevski's, the president and founder of *Economica*. It was at the end of dinner that Jean-François threw out the idea of this book on the "psychology of battle." What did you have in mind?

Phelizon – For a long time, I had noticed that there was an abundance of literature on the technique of chess, but there didn't seem to be anything on the psychology of the game. And in my opinion, Anatoly is the one grand champion chess player who is the master of its psychological aspect. For my part, I had always noticed that in the business world and more broadly in all negotiations, it's precisely the psychological aspects that are the most important. Actually, all negotiations are a "game" just like a chess match. By game, I mean that the universe of negotiation is closer to the world of chess than of war. Both adversaries must follow a certain number of rules. This is not the case in war where most *normal* rules are abolished and where an imperative need to kill is invoked.

That is why the term "economic warfare" seems to me to be totally inappropriate. In the business world, naturally there is fighting, but there is no war. Consequently, you should never consider your adversary an enemy. A negotiation will never come to fruition as long as a common ground of understanding with the other party cannot be found. This point can never be forgotten.

So, a negotiator will have no hesitation resorting to the Japanese concept of *nemawashi*.[8] He knows how to create personal relationships with the participants so he can establish, sometimes informally, as many points of agreement as possible.

Incidentally, it is good to prepare topics of conversation for the *break* periods. Topics are endless: studies, family, vacation, cars, even golf. You have a better chance of succeeding by engaging your adversary in conversation than by being condescending and aloof. You should also make an effort to appear approachable. You should open up somewhat to elicit a little friendship; however, not so much that you seem transparent.

Karpov – It is clear that chess is not a *model* for the military world, the business world, or the political world. Why? Because in chess, the pieces always start from the same positions. Consequently, each player's chances of winning are more or less the same. His skill and ability will make the difference. In the real world, however, it is extremely rare to find a balanced starting situation where the chances of winning for both parties are about equal.

That being said, the study of the psychology of chess can offer useful parallels in general to someone in business or politics. First, the number of possible combinations in chess is immense.[9] Even the most powerful computers cannot calculate all the variations. That is how things are in real life. The combinations are infinite and situations cannot be reduced to equations. Chess is not a science but an art. Or, as I often say, chess is "an art, a science, and a sport."

A second similarity between chess and the business world relates to the uncertainty that the protagonists face with the future. At some point during the confrontation, the adversary holds a decisive advantage. But, his attention might drift; he might lose concentration. Actually, he believes in his heart that the game is over. But as we were discussing, anything can happen until the score sheet is signed. In other words, even when victory is only moments away, nothing is assured.

Phelizon – Yes, everyone knows that it's the last 100 meters of a race that are the hardest to run.

A GAME THAT BELONGS TO ALL[10]

It's true that I knew firsthand the mysterious attraction of this royal game, the only game invented by man that escapes the tyranny of accident, the only one where you owe your victory to your intelligence only, or more precisely, to a form of intelligence. But isn't it highly unfair to call chess a game? Isn't it also a science, an art, or something else that, like the coffin of Mahomet between heaven and earth, is suspended between one and the other, and embraces an incredible number of contradictions?

Its origin is lost in the dawn of time, but is forever new. Its process is mechanical, but only shows results thanks to the imagination; it is closely limited by a fixed geometric space but its combinations are limitless. It follows a continuous development but stays sterile; it's a thought that leads nowhere, mathematics that establish nothing, an art that leaves no work, an architecture without matter. Yet is more durable, in its way, than books, or any other monument, this singular game for all people and all times, a gift from which god no one knows, to alleviate boredom, to sharpen the spirit, and to stimulate the soul.

Where does it begin, and where does it end? A child can learn the basic rules, a neophyte can try his hand at it and within the limited square of the board acquire a unique kind of mastery if he has received the special gift. Patience, a sudden vision, and technique join in very specific proportions to make discoveries, as in mathematics, poetry, or music—by perhaps simply mixing them a different way.

In a negotiation, it isn't the signing of the agreement that represents the last 100 meters but the cashing of the check. That's why a transaction cannot be deemed concluded until payment has been made.

Karpov – I would like to mention a third point. On a chessboard in each camp, there are thirty-two pieces of unequal value. The pawns don't look like much and often they are considered of negligible importance. These pieces however are very precious; they are the soul of chess as Philidor[11] used to say.

They defend and support more prestigious pieces like the bishop or the knight, who in turn support and defend the king and the queen.

But aren't there pawns in everyday life? Don't they support the intermediate levels, and finally the entire command structure?

I think so. And I think that the position of the king depends on whether the positions of the pawns are strong or not.

Kouatly – In real life, it is true that the pawns often make the difference.

Karpov – Well, in any case, they're the ones who do all the work.

Phelizon – In chess as in any negotiation process, the goal is to put in place the elements of a "battle logic." Tactics in the end are universal. Or more accurately, it transcends disciplines and situations. But this logic responds to other, more *emotional* considerations like the protagonists' temperaments, what they like and dislike, or the strategists' desire to successfully implement the strategies they've defined.

Which means, parenthetically, that if software programs can in some instances help make a decision, they are certainly insufficient, for they cannot grasp what I call the "psychological profile of the opponent." Actually, it is almost impossible to win a battle or lead a negotiation without *first* making the effort to understand what your opponent wants.

Karpov – Yes, it seems to me that as important as it is, an analysis of the conflict is not enough to win. It is absolutely necessary—of that I'm sure—but the mechanics of a battle cannot be rationalized 100 percent.

Kouatly – Of course, everyday life isn't the same thing as a game of chess. However, there are more similarities than differences in how to fight a chess game and negotiate an agreement, or more generally lead a battle.

This little book aims to show the importance of psychological factors in confrontational situations. We will start by discussing the battle preparation phase. Then we will study the different possible approaches: the power approach, direct or indirect, and the lateral approach. Finally, we will explore what comes after the battle.

Naturally, Anatoly and Jean-François won't be discussing the psychology of battle strictly from a theoretical viewpoint. They will constantly refer to concrete experiences or famous examples from the history of chess, literature, or history in general.

CHAPTER 1

Preparing for Battle

Physical preparation: eat, sleep, exercise, stay local. – Preparing intellectually. – Know the opponent's history, psychological profile. – Make a list of absolute priorities. – Don't go into it alone. – Neutralize the opponent's advantages. – Advancing on the road to agreement. – Scoring early success. – Effect of surprise. – Role of time in play and negotiations.

Researching facts is the nerve of all negotiation.
Richard M. Nixon

Kouatly – Before thinking about going to battle, you must first prepare. The same applies to negotiating. You must be prepared. Should the importance of preparation be proportionate to the size of the stakes?

Phelizon – Unfortunately, the higher the stakes, the more responsibility you are usually carrying. Therefore you often have less time to get prepared. A major negotiation always comes in addition to all the other myriad routine items that still need to be dealt with, even after delegating as much as possible, of course.

     In the business world, it is very common that the main negotiator holds a very important position within his company: he's the CEO or CFO. That isn't good, since it means that he can't concentrate 100 percent on what he's doing. Naturally, he has other things on his mind: managers to meet, investment decisions to make, plants to visit, results to publish, analysts to convince, etc. Ideally, a negotiation should be the negotiator's full-time job. But he should hold a position of enough responsibility that he can speak for his company.

Kouatly – Anatoly, how do you physically prepare for a tournament? Are you careful about your sleeping requirements, your nutrition?

Karpov – Physical preparation is extremely important for a chess player and—I suspect also—in the worlds of business and politics.

I am often surprised at how little attention businesspeople or diplomats devote to this aspect of physical preparation. In all these arenas, they need to concentrate for long periods of time in difficult and sometimes hostile environments. Only a perfectly fit person can stand such concentration under that kind of pressure.

In the chess world, I think that Botvinnik was the first one to stress the importance of physical preparation before a tournament. Throughout his entire life, Botvinnik took great care of himself. Fortunately, he enjoyed excellent health and his form was dazzling. He was still world champion at forty-six.

During the 1950s, being concerned with physical preparation was a brand new concept. Fortunately, medicine quickly supported this sport of chess. Scientists started doing tests during the Tel Aviv chess tournaments and continued during the Tokyo chess tournaments. They were quite surprised to see that the Russian chess team was very athletic and was in excellent health. Even if the players didn't excel at any particular sport, they all jogged, worked out, skied, swam, and did gymnastics. For myself, I ski, swim, and do gymnastics. I also started playing tennis.

Kouatly – So, the scientists realized that the better physical condition the player is in, the better his chances of winning tournaments. Has the same realization been made in business?

Phelizon – No, doctors don't perform this type of study and gyms are not a common sight in most corporate locations—except maybe in California. There must be, however, a correlation between physical condition and performance, especially when dealing with a difficult negotiation. Since all essentially intellectual battles play out also on the physical level, you can only recommend to a negotiating team to drink little, get enough sleep, reduce caffeine consumption, and, if possible, get some exercise.

Let's not forget that "*wearing out the opponent*" is an effective tactic that deserves consideration. History has lost count of the number of defeats that are the direct result of the exhaustion of the leaders or their troops. On that issue, the repeated effects of jet lag can turn out to be disastrous. Anyone can see that an "intercontinental" negotiation (and by that I mean one between an American team and a European or Asian team) takes a completely different course depending on whether the meetings always take place at the same location or not. For example, if every week an American team must spend a day negotiating in Europe, it will eventually concede more to the opposing team than if the meeting locations alternate between Europe and the United States. So, not coincidentally, English bankers insist that all meetings take place in London.

If you want to acquire a company in Europe and you are based in the United States, try to cross the Atlantic as little as possible. Ask your opposing negotiating team to come to the United States. If they accept, don't hesitate to entertain them at the finest restaurants. You will reap the benefits. If they refuse, then just tell them that to be fair, the location of the meetings should alternate. Naturally, you should try to negotiate the points that are important to you when you have the home advantage. This way you will have at least created a certain balance between the teams.

Of course, if you agree to always travel, you will be handicapping yourself. It's easy to imagine the physical condition of the American who after eight or ten hours of flight and six or eight hours of time zone difference arrives in Europe and sits down immediately to the negotiating table—or in front of a chessboard.

Karpov – Naturally, he's completely out of it. He eats anything and drinks cup after cup of coffee to keep going. But coffee isn't enough to remain alert. After this type of treatment, a person doesn't really know where he is. He can even have trouble correctly appreciating the situation in which he finds himself.

Phelizon – Let me add that it's always better to negotiate after a meal. By this, I mean a meal where your opponent eats and drinks well, whereas you have barely sipped at your wine. Anyone will notice that ideas are clearer when you're hungry and that you're more aggressive. Conversely, you are more flexible after a good meal and less likely to want to fight.

Karpov – One day, I was playing a match in London and the organizers had invited Margaret Thatcher to the opening ceremony. She and I had the chance to talk for a few moments. She told me that the most difficult political debates she had were in Parliament and she added, "When I go to Parliament, I never eat a thing. In the morning I have a cup of coffee or tea. I concentrate better and my reactions are quicker when on an empty stomach."

In chess, a game can last a long time (five hours, for example). You must always remember that if you eat too much before the game, your game will not be very aggressive, especially at the beginning. On the other hand, if you don't eat enough, you risk losing your abilities by the end of the match, for lack of energy.

Kouatly – Fighting a battle demands patience, determination, endurance (hence the importance of physical conditioning)—and a certain sense of humor. But physical preparation isn't enough. You must also prepare intellectually, which is much more difficult.

Karpov – Intellectual preparation for chess is difficult and complicated. Many different factors come into play because the players themselves are very different from each other. The most important point concerns information in general. First, you need to know everything going on in the world of chess. Only then can you establish your repertoire of openings and decide which positions are favorable for you and not your opponent.

It's strange, but sometimes you start a game without giving yourself all the advantages. For example, your right wing (the king's wing) may be excellent but so is your opponent's left wing (the queen's wing) and you find yourself almost even again. That's when you feel like concentrating on a different area of the game, where you think your opponent isn't as strong as you are. Your position may not be ideal, but you feel it's better than his. You can't consider this change of tactic without having deeply studied your opponent's game and habits, as well as the history of your own games as well.

This entire preparation phase amounts to what Jean-François called the opponent's "psychological profile." Then it's up to you to adapt to this portrait using your own talents. In the final analysis, you must define your game plan, as much by using some of the teachings that have impressed you as by the adverse reactions you can anticipate.

THE GAME PLAN[1]

At the core of chess strategy is what is called the game plan. It is difficult to play a game calculating only one or two moves in advance. From the opening, the player has a specified game plan for a specified time and tries to stick to it.

Circumstances and situation changes on the board force him to correct the initial plan, sometimes giving it up to adopt another plan. Normally, you change plans when you go from one stage of a game to another, especially when you get to the final moves.

Practice shows that the chosen opening determines the game plan, or more precisely, the structure of the pawns at the beginning. The realization of this plan comes in the middle of the game. Usually, you have a separate plan for the final moves. Therefore, the plan plays an important role: it is the link between the opening and the middle of the game.

In order to have a successful strategy in chess, or as it's called a *positional game*, you must know how to choose an action plan, move your pieces precisely, and anticipate the moves to come.

As to tactics, or *combination game*, the player is faced with localized confrontations. The precise analysis of the variables, a clear understanding of the position, and the possession of an arsenal of technical means then take on their full importance.

Kouatly – Of course, your opponent might also be tempted to put together your psychological profile.

Karpov – You should definitely assume that he is doing the same analysis on you as you have done on him. So, he could certainly guess what you plan to do. But if he stresses you or puts you under pressure, you will need to adapt, modify your tactical moves, and perhaps even change your game plan. The decisions you then make should be based on your knowledge of your opponent's psychological profile.

Phelizon – Being prepared is compiling facts, believing in principles, and establishing priorities. Compiling facts means not just numbers but an intimate knowledge of the opponent: his motivation, his organization, his likely objectives. Believing in principles shouldn't be confused with taking a position. Groucho Marx used to say, "Here are my principles. If you don't like them, I can change." You shouldn't fall into that trap. Pragmatism applies to tactical positions and moves. Principles should remain unchanged and always indicate the path you follow. Priorities can only be established in relation to principles.

Before starting to negotiate, you should make two lists: one with points you won't relinquish under any circumstance, and one with points that you want to obtain from the opponent. The first list contains absolute priorities, which if not satisfied, become deal breakers. The second list contains negotiable priorities. Absolute priorities are often satisfied by easing up on the negotiable priorities.

When preparing mentally, you must let go of all arrogance and all naïveté. To *be humble to the experience* is truly the supreme commandment of the mind. Let's remember La Fontaine making fun of that arrogant and naïve rooster: "I think this is a fine pearl," he says as he shows it to the jeweler, "but the smallest grain of wheat would be more to my liking."[2] It is simply preferable not to go into battle when you *think you know.* To be content to think you know can be fatal. So, preparing mentally means being sure, sure of the opponent's situation, his positions, and intentions.

Kouatly – Can you sometimes overestimate your opponent?

Phelizon – Yes, of course. When I say be sure, I should specify, be sure of the actual strengths of the situation and the motivations in play. Nothing is worse than a false certainty. It can make you commit the most serious mistakes. Therefore, never forget that the other party may not be as well prepared as you are. That perhaps he doesn't know you as well as you think. That his vision of priorities and objectives may not be as clear as yours.

Kouatly – But all the certainties you mention refer mostly to the past.

Phelizon – Yes and knowing past facts, obviously, is not enough. But who would buy a company without doing an in-depth due diligence? Who would wage a battle without checking to see how the opponent's forces are aligned? Who would start a fight without considering the strengths or weaknesses of the opponent? Jesse Unruh, one of Richard Nixon's political adversaries, was the Speaker of the House of Representatives and would often say that money is the nerve of politics. "Well," said Nixon one day, "I would like to paraphrase Jesse and say that researching facts is the nerve of all negotiation."[3] In reality, if mental preparation can help determine the strength you're facing, as precisely as possible, on all levels, it will minimize any potential effect of surprise by your opponent.

Kouatly – Let's assume that you are determined not to let yourself be led by your ego. Therefore you are not obsessed with being right.

You know the objective you're going after. You're familiar with not only your research, but also with what motivates the person you're speaking with and how the opposing organization functions. You have a clear vision of your principles and priorities. Finally, you've created two lists: one for required elements and one for desired elements. Are you ready?

Karpov – No, not yet, because you never go into the fight alone. A back room is always necessary. In the past, at world championships, the support teams were made up of a half-dozen technicians whose job it was to analyze the games and do research. But I was an innovator and added a cook and a psychologist. I thought that the cook was an important element to the team, not only because championships lasted a long time (two or three months), but also because analysis and research can take place at all hours of the day or night. You also have to factor in the time zone difference and the vagaries of hotel cooking that more often than not is absolutely inadequate. The cook therefore was supposed to satisfy all the culinary needs of the team, at any time, at their request.

Naturally, the first time I asked to include a cook on the team (it was for a championship that I was playing in the Philippines), I had some difficulty justifying it to the Soviet administration. After much discussion with the Federation and the Ministry of Sport, an inspector finally came to Manila to see the situation for himself. He noted that I had a comfortable apartment in a five-star hotel, and that the hotel had a Japanese restaurant, a Filipino restaurant, and even a French restaurant.

"So, why do you need to add a cook?" he asked, a little annoyed. I told him that the food at the hotel was excellent for inspectors and tourists but that it didn't suit people who were playing a world chess championship. "In addition," I said, "the hour before a game is very important. You need extreme concentration. You can't be wasting energy calling back room service that hasn't arrived." And I prevailed.

Kouatly – Why add a psychologist?

Karpov – This was in 1974 in Moscow. Viktor Korchnoi, a player I knew well, was my opponent. I knew that it was very important for him to feel that he had an "advantage." But what was this advantage?

During the third game, I realized that someone in the crowd kept staring at me. I had no idea what his strange looks meant. But I could feel this man looking at me all the time, when I played, when I was thinking, when I got up, and when I walked around the stage. After the game, I asked my trainer who this strange person was who had almost disrupted me. He responded that it was Korchnoi's psychologist.

I immediately decided that I had to neutralize this "advantage" Korchnoi had given himself. I decided to incorporate a psychologist in my team also. I called my doctor in Leningrad. He said my request wouldn't be easy to satisfy. Then, he remembered that among his friends when he was a medical student, there was one who became a psychologist and was assisting Russian cosmonauts. "I think he works on sleep disorders." He added, "He's a real scientist. He lives in Moscow." I asked him to get in contact with him, which he did. The following day, the psychologist called me. I spoke with him at length and he agreed to join us without delay.

Obviously, it wasn't really for me that I added this new advisor. Psychologically speaking, I am solid. It was more to show Korchnoi that by covering this psychological component he had lost his "advantage."

Since then, my psychologist has attended many of my matches and has become very well known in the chess world.

Kouatly – It has often been said that Korchnoi employed not only psychologists but also parapsychologists.

Karpov – Yes, but I don't think they were very useful to him. In any case, I've never had any use for that kind of person.

Kouatly – Are there also psychologists on mergers and acquisitions negotiating teams?

Phelizon – No, absolutely not, but perhaps that's a shame. Naturally, all negotiators are supposed to use psychology to some extent, but how much? It probably would be a very good idea to ask a professional who is adept at observing and deciphering behavior to report to the negotiating team leader between sessions: to tell him how his offer is received, if he feels the opponent is bluffing, how he sees the roles being played out within the opposing team. I can imagine the benefit he could bring, not only in assisting but in creating a certain unease within the other team. I like this idea and maybe someday I can test it.

Kouatly – It would be a good example of cross fertilization between the business world and the chess world, but in your opinion what is the ideal composition of the usual back office?

Phelizon – I would say that the ideal team is made up of an advisor (someone who is trustworthy and challenging or who can interject common sense), accountants able to pick apart not only what the finance department has recorded, but all the rest (contingent and off balance sheet), a business lawyer backed by a solid technical team, and a banker, especially if there are financing problems (often the advisor is the lawyer or the banker).

But, putting together a good team isn't enough. You must also observe the opposing team and even "tag" them. And you should never forget that your best potential ally is the opposing team's advisor.

Kouatly – What do you mean by that?

Phelizon – Sometimes the negotiating process gets blocked. Neither side is willing to budge from its position and everything is at a standstill. They might even have realized they faced a serious disagreement. A good way to unblock the situation is for one of the advisors to send a message to his counterpart saying something like, "If your client would be willing to accept this point of contention, then perhaps mine would be willing to let go of this one." These unofficial exchanges are very important because they help determine what is essential to the opposing party, or better, to understand what they'll never accept.

Kouatly – All combat follows rules—and if possible, the rules are accepted by both sides. By that I mean written rules, naturally, but also other implicit rules, often imposed by the players themselves.

Karpov – The rules specific to chess are obviously known to all. What is less known, however, are the rules governing tournaments, and some of these are more or less explicit.

In world championships there are always many details to settle between the two players. One of the camps will sometimes even try to modify the rules to their advantage. That was the case with Fischer, who tried a little too often to change tournament rules.[4] In 1975 in particular, since he likes tropical countries, he wanted a Southeast Asian country, the Philippines, to host the championships. He must have known how allergic I am to hot and humid climates. He also insisted that the reigning world champion need only hold a two-point difference with the challenger to keep his title. Obviously, this wasn't acceptable and since he dug into his position, the championship did not take place and he lost his title.

Kouatly – I think once in Reykjavik, Fischer was so suspicious that he insisted on opening the envelopes determining the color choice for the first game. After that he continued to make diva-like requests, from details on the strength of the indirect lighting to emptying the first nine rows because the spectators bothered him.

Phelizon – The business world also has its rules. And I don't just mean the laws and regulations that are imposed on all business leaders. But rather, I would like to elaborate a little on the implicit rules that all parties present in a negotiation usually respect.

Negotiating is advancing on the road to agreement. But an agreement isn't reduced to a "yes" or a "no." It's made up of all kinds of clauses. One of the first implicit rules is that you do not renege on a point that has been accepted. At the very least, it would be unfair.

The second rule is more of an ethics consideration. There exists a business ethic where some things are not acceptable. Some of the things that are strictly forbidden by the code of ethics and in general by the establishment are as follows: conducting fictitious negotiations to obtain information; stealing plans or confidential documents; and spying on the offices or homes of your opponent, thereby threatening his privacy. In most Western countries, these actions are severely dealt with by courts of law.

I would like to add something that is often forgotten: when you are the seller, usually you can only modify the asking price downward. And when you are the buyer, usually you can only modify the purchase price upward. To deviate from this common sense attitude would not be negotiating in good faith and could certainly constitute a deal breaker.

Apart from this commonly accepted ethical code, all else is fair game, naturally. Among accepted practices would be speaking with the clients and suppliers of the other company, analyzing the quality of its products and services, studying financial reports and research documents, or even "turning" some of its managers.

THE MOMENT THE ACCOMPLISHED PLAYER AWAITS[5]

Negotiations always start with a period of great confusion. The outcome is far from certain—each party tries to obtain a lot and asks for more than is reasonable with the expectation of having to give up some things in the future. Various demands come to light, whose only purpose is to test the opponent's position. It is only after a time, when the main thrusts of the parties present are exposed, that a clearer and much more delicate phase begins, one during which the outcome will be decided. Everyone has already given up what they were resigned to lose and refused what they were determined not to accept at any price. All that remains is the loose and imprecise problem of the other issues that will be shared. This is the moment the accomplished player waits for.

Kouatly – Do the rules apply equally to both parties present?

Phelizon – Usually, yes. But what Anatoly was saying about Fischer can also be seen in some negotiations. By that I mean the upper hand that some sides try to gain by making demands. When the owner of a business enters into a discussion with the representatives of a tech company, both parties are not really playing on the same field. That's how when Nelson Pelz sold Triangle to Péchiney or Barry Diller sold USA Networks to Vivendi, the natural advantage of a member of the "jet set" over an ordinary salaried manager probably biased certain behaviors. It is true that deals were made, but the sellers definitely had the advantage.

When one side is in a position to dazzle the other with yachts and private jets, you can't really say that the rules of the game are even.

Kouatly – This is the heart of the psychological aspect of battle. Doesn't the one who succeeds in "impressing" the other have victory in sight?

Karpov – In chess, we say that the hardest thing to establish and maintain is a "winning position." It's hard to maintain because a reversal of the situation is always possible. If you hesitate to take advantage of a winning position, your opponent can take the advantage back, especially by regrouping his forces to the rear. That's when you run the risk of losing your advantage.

Phelizon – In the business world, the advantage an opponent takes over the other can be the result of different factors. I mentioned personal fortune, which might make the most seasoned executives lose their head. Experience is another important factor. I would like to tell the story of the aborted meeting which took place at the beginning of 1939, between a French-British delegation and a Soviet delegation. Had this meeting been successful, the U.S.S.R. might have entered World War II long before 1942.

These are the words of General Beaufre: "The Soviet delegation, used to working in committees through its government role in the Russian state, had much more experience in the kind of negotiating in which we were about to engage. It was noticeable at the very first session, where Marshal Vorochilov[6] immediately asked a few questions relating to process: agenda, presidency, minutes, powers; all issues well known to the Russians and to which it appeared we had given no thought. Therefore, we agreed to all his proposals. This was all strictly routine, but Vorochilov, already quite at ease, was emerging as the leader of the discussions.

The question of verification of powers gave him another chance to score a success. He rose and solemnly read a document indicating that the Soviet mission had the power to sign military treaties for peace and against aggression; he then asked the other heads of mission to present their powers. General Doumenc presented his mission orders indicating that he was authorized to treat all military issues. This vague expression fortunately contained the word 'treat,' which in a larger sense could seem to have the same value as Marshal Vorochilov's powers.

When it came to Admiral Drax, he had to admit after much hesitation that he had no written powers, but that it must seem evident to Marshal Vorochilov that the British government wouldn't have sent him without any real powers, even though he actually had no document."

This story shows once more that if both parties are not on equal footing, the negotiation can only be biased.

Kouatly – We have seen that an upper hand can give the decisive advantage. Surprise can also. As the saying goes, "A surprised man is a man half defeated."

Phelizon – It is undeniable that an attack is more efficient when coupled with the effect of surprise. Napoleon would not have won the battle of Austerlitz without the surprise effect caused by Murat's charge. It is also clear what effect a surprise attack can have on public opinion. I am reminded of Pearl Harbor or the terrorist attack on September 11, 2001, in New York. The same applies to the business world. If you say to one of your competitors from the onset, "Name your price. I'm going to buy you regardless," that can have more effect than subtle and lengthy approach maneuvers.

Let's say that surprise, because it disorients the opponent, acts as a catalyst to victory.

Kouatly – Can a surprise be impromptu or does it need to be carefully prepared?

Karpov – It should be prepared well in advance and kept a secret. I remember in 1987 in Seville, Kasparov used an opening that I wasn't expecting but that I knew well, having prepared a variation of it a few years earlier. Strangely enough, Kasparov must have been surprised, judging by the fact that he thought for over an hour and a half for the first ten moves.

Phelizon – I would like to refer for a moment to the Chinese tradition that distinguishes ordinary strength (*zheng*) from extraordinary strength (*qi*)[7]. The first one enables you to contain your adversary— for example by encircling him—and the second one to distract him— for example by flanking him. A *zheng* move is relatively predictable. It conforms to the order of things. But a *qi* move is unpredictable, surprising, or contrary to the norm.

In *The Art of War*, Sun Tzu suggests attacking with the *zheng* and winning with the *qi*. For him, diversion moves are almost always required and you must always have some in reserve. These are the moves that enable you to deal the winning blow, right where the opponent feels no threat or is not prepared. Sun Tzu compares the two forces, *zheng* and *qi*, to two intertwined rings. "Who can say," he writes, "where one starts and the other ends?"[8]

Therefore, the interchangeable use of these strengths offers an infinite variety of possibilities. Surprise can also come from an attack in force that the enemy considers unlikely. But this combination of strengths has consequences on how to conduct a battle; even when you consider a frontal attack, you must always carefully prepare for one or more diversion moves.

Kouatly – How can you create a surprise effect in chess when everything is "on the table"?

Karpov – You can create a surprise, for example, by choosing a disconcerting opening. I must explain the word "disconcerting." Experienced chess players know all the possible openings and there are no new ones. But they prefer some to others. This means they have their little habits, which of course are well known to their opponents. The surprise can come precisely from the fact that you've added a variation to your usual repertoire of opening moves. You can use it knowing that it will "displease" your opponent. By showing him that you are well aware of what he likes and doesn't like, you have a good chance of taking him by surprise.

Naturally, if you've prepared something new, you must know how to choose your moment: when everyone is a little tired, when the teams need rest, etc. By creating surprise, you will force the team to analyze at the worst possible moment what you intend to do. Is this a new strategy you're implementing? Is this a diversion move? Is it merely a move designed to provoke? The team will have to work very hard to understand and then find a countermove, and that's how you will be able to get the advantage. I'm sure that in business, this kind of tactic is widely used.

THE MOMENT OF UNCERTAINTY[9]

I've always noticed that in negotiating, the element of surprise is a valuable asset for those who know how to use it. Each team comes with a set of ideas and arguments established in advance. There is nothing in their plan that hasn't been turned over and examined twenty times. So, anything new, even favorable, disrupts this preconceived order and creates a moment of uncertainty, which the quicker mind uses to his advantage before the others.

Kouatly – Therefore, it is because the element of surprise breaks the concentration or disconcerts that it can create success.

Phelizon – Yes, surprise is nothing other than a *creator of uncertainty*. Many tactical successes are the result of the opponent's uncertainty. It is clear that a faulty analysis of the situation increases de facto the condition of uncertainty in which you find yourself, and that an accurate analysis reduces that uncertainty. Because it creates trouble with the opponent's analysis, surprise leads them to indecision or bad decisions. Indecision creates irresolution.

Kouatly – Isn't launching a hostile takeover a typical surprise move?

Phelizon – Yes, of course. When buying a company, the executives of the company in play often adopt a warlike attitude. Henry IV said that you had to be the hammer or the anvil. In most financial transactions (mergers and acquisitions), it is the same. You are either the hunter or the hunted. You need to establish a position of hunter, predator, or attacker. From that standpoint, a hostile takeover is nothing more than a duel requiring careful planning, very diverse talents, sufficient financial means, and which in the end, is won by surprise.

   Sometimes the announcement of a hostile takeover destabilizes the executive team to such an extent that they are incapable of counterattacking. The company I work for once decided to buy a British company, through a hostile takeover if necessary. Our banker called the company's board members on a Saturday afternoon to advise them of our intentions. As you can imagine, many financial transactions happen during the weekend. Of course, the board members were very surprised by this move.

   In any case, an appointment was made for the following evening in London. The meeting began in a very hostile environment. "This is our offer," we announced to the board of the targeted company. "Considering the current stock market value, we consider it reasonable. Either you accept it, and within the framework of a friendly takeover we proceed to the discussion of some practical issues of interest to you, or you turn it down and we launch a hostile takeover for the company. It will be up to you then to explain to your shareholders why you didn't consider our offer." (In Great Britain, directors are held responsible if they refuse an offer that fairly assesses the company they represent.) After many breaks in the session, an agreement was finally reached at 4:00 AM. The operation lasted less than thirty-six hours.

Kouatly – In order to surprise the enemy, the time factor needs to be managed. This is crucial in chess since the game has a specific time limit.

Karpov – Time not only comes into play during a game, but before and after a game throughout the two or three months that a tournament lasts. You could say that a game is to a negotiating session what a tournament is to the entire negotiation.

Using your time wisely between each session is critical, for that's when both teams analyze what just took place and prepare for the next sessions. They pick apart the opponent's strategy, try to understand his past and future reactions, advise the player, and even guide his decisions.

So for me, time is a little like the third player in the game. Time can be an ally or an adversary; it all depends on where you stand. In the business world, it seems to me that time is more often an ally, because you can always decide later. In chess, that is not the case. Having time as an ally is more difficult.

Kouatly – What do you mean by that?

Karpov – First you have to ask this very simple question: "Am I in charge of this situation short-term?" or to put it otherwise "Do I have time or not?" When time is of the essence, you cannot try to analyze. You can only count on your intuition and experience. So, rapid play chess requires completely different abilities than classic chess. It is somewhat like in the business world, when you don't really have a lot of time to think, but you "see," meaning you know, that a decision needs to be made. You don't try to find the best solution, or make the best decision. It would be better if you could take the time to do the research but you can't because you would lose precious time.

When on the other hand you are not constrained by time, you have the freedom to consider the situation long term. You can examine the ins and outs and make totally informed choices or make the best decision with all the facts.

ZADIG WAS RIGHT[10]

The great magician first asked this question: What is the longest and shortest of things in the world, the fastest and the slowest, the easiest to divide and the vastest, the most neglected and the most regretted, without which nothing can be done, that devours all that is small and revives all that is big? Itabad was the first to speak and said a man like him did not understand enigmas and it was enough for him to win with his spear. Some said the answer was fortune, others the earth, still others said light. Zadig told them it was time. And he added, nothing is longer since it measures eternity; nothing is shorter since we never have enough for our projects; nothing is slower to one who waits; nothing is faster to one who enjoys; it can be as big as infinity and be divided infinitely; all men neglect it, and regret its loss; nothing is done without it; it makes you forget what is unworthy of posterity and immortalizes great things. The assembly agreed that Zadig was right.

Managing time is also sequencing events. In today's chess tournaments, any game started must be finished within the day. That was not the case in the old days. When a game was adjourned it was extremely important to choose your final position. If your move was obvious, it was better to make it. But if you faced a difficult choice, with three or four options heavy with consequences that you were considering, it was better to suspend the game and use the coming night to analyze the possible options in detail with your advisors.

On our team, we always respected the following rule: at adjournment time, if you were holding a "winning position," you should suspend the game as quickly as possible. But if you weren't in a "winning position," you should hold on as long as possible. I think that Botvinnik was the first to formulate that rule.

Kouatly – And it seems to me this rule transfers as is to negotiations.

Phelizon – It's obvious that it is better to suspend a session when you've just won an important point. And the contrary is also true that you should be ready to prolong discussions when you feel you are getting nowhere.

The logic of the give and take can be very subtle. Often you fight for a minor point, not because you really care, but because you want to trick your opponent into thinking that it is really important to you. The other side starts to wonder why, and little by little concentrates on this issue that seems close to your heart. That's when you can start to make your offer.

In exchange for this minor point that you will give up with much regret, you insist on obtaining another point in contention, which actually is very important to you and that you casually put on the table. This is the heart of the seventeenth stratagem ("throwing a brick to pick up jade").[11]

Karpov – I've experienced that kind of situation, not at a chessboard, but when discussing conditions and details of a tournament. You don't give a fig for one point, but you know you are going to run into problems elsewhere. So you pretend to give in on a point that is of no importance to you—you give in while pretending to do your opponent a favor—but it's only to gain the advantage in the upcoming discussion.

Kouatly – I wonder if the preparation phase of a battle might just boil down to always giving yourself room to maneuver, in other words having options to trade.

Phelizon – Preparing means establishing rules, defining your tactics, but also remaining flexible, just like water which always finds a way to run downhill.

For me, strategic action derives from the direction imposed on the entire group, and in that sense, strategy is nothing more than a collective rule. On the other hand, tactical action must be continuously adapted to the actions, movements, and plans of the enemy as they are discovered. In other words, it must remain fluid and unpredictable whatever the circumstances. What characterizes strategy therefore is continuity, whereas what characterizes tactics is flexibility.

I think this distinction between strategy and tactics is essential and should serve as the foundation of any battle or war. In any case, it seems to me much more pertinent than the classic definitions of strategy and tactics that are in a way *dovetailed*: "the organization of a military operation" for one and "the execution of a military operation" for the other. In reality, tactics is not a smaller part of strategy. It is just a different essence.

CHAPTER 2

Select a Style and Approach

Confrontational style. – Concessionary style. – Provocation
as a tool. – Concession vs. submission. – Direct or frontal
approach: warlike behavior. – Indirect or oblique approach:
more efficient, less immediate. – Lateral approach: most
subtle. – Fool you twice. – Conciliatory resistance. – Keeping
the energy up. – Risk of the direct approach.

You should never let your enemy feel the weak side, where with a little pressure,
the sword can pierce.
C. A. Saint-Beuve

Kouatly – When you start to fight, determination, endurance, and knowledge of the environment make the difference. Even allowing for sufficient battle preparation, you still have to determine a style and an approach.

Phelizon – I think two styles and three approaches can be distinguished. What is a style? That's what results from the personalities of the protagonists, rarely from the circumstances in which they find themselves.

To make it simple, I would say there is a confrontational style and a concessionary (nonconfrontational) style. The first describes people who always want to get something without giving anything in exchange. The second describes those who are always ready to offer something in exchange for what they want. Naturally, you can find crossovers in these two styles. Sometimes, depending on circumstances, a person might be confrontational or offer compromise in turn. But more often than not, these styles denote a personality trait.

Confrontational people tend to bring all the discussions back to their point of view, without trying to understand or even listen to the others. They seek to defeat their opponent rather than convince him. They never forget that *less* for the opponent means *more* for them and *more* for the opponent means *less* for them. They won't hesitate to bluff, dramatize, impose their conditions, retract themselves, intimidate, threaten, or bully. They actually often cover their inflexibility with aggression.

On the contrary, the compromising personality prefers to re-center the discussions into a long-term perspective, without ever sacrificing the essentials. They will always try to listen and understand, at the risk of not disclosing their intentions. They will strive to convince you that *more* for you can also translate to *more* for them, and *less* for them to *less* for you. They will try to put you at ease, use humor, make your life easier, take good care of you, in a phrase "put you in their pocket."

At the risk of simplifying things, every time you make a demand without offering anything in exchange, you provoke the other party and come closer to a confrontational style. Every time you make an offer without asking for anything in exchange, you submit to the other party and come closer to a concessionary style.

Kouatly – It seems to me that the very nature of chess makes it confrontational since the object is to defeat your opponent. Conversely, the nature of negotiation must be conciliatory since you must reach an agreement with your adversary.

Karpov – Some chess champions enjoy provocation. Botvinnik was particularly aggressive. Kasparov[1] and Korchnoi are also, but a little less than Botvinnik. It feels like they have to unleash torrents of hate for their opponent to be at the peak of their form. I guess a boxer might act the same.

At the other extreme, there is Spassky. He hates confrontation. His best games are the ones he played against opponents who were his friends. I would put all the other champions between those extremes represented by Botvinnik and Spassky. For my part, I have no trouble finding myself across from a player who likes to provoke. I have to say that I don't enjoy playing against a friend as much, since I know that if I win it will affect him.

Kouatly – When you are being challenged, it's always easier to face an enemy than a friend.

Karpov – Jean-François said that in the business world, you fight, but you never wage war and that you should never think of your opponent as the enemy. In the chess world it is the same thing. There are no enemies, there are merely opponents. I can have a good or a bad relationship with a given player, but that's not important, for he is never an enemy. The only thing that bothers me, as I've said, is playing against one of my true friends.

So, it's not having a "friend" or an "enemy" across the board from me that changes anything. Rather it's having someone you know well professionally, or not well at all.

Spassky played many times against Petrosian[2] and knew him well. One day he told me he knew exactly when Petrosian was about to launch an attack on the board. Petrosian couldn't help himself from stalking quietly around the stage like a tiger ready to pounce on his prey.

Kouatly – Isn't provocation a tactic often used by negotiators?

Phelizon – Of course. During a negotiation, you want to try to get the opposing party off balance, provoke him. Anger will certainly make him commit a mistake. By appeasing him afterward, you can lead him more easily to your point of view.

Conversely, you must be careful not to respond to his provocation. He's probably trying to make you lose control. In that case, you need to try to bring the discussion back into the framework of what you've said before. But be careful not to say more than you already did.

Of course, you can decide to be as aggressive as he is or perhaps even more. Your behavior might calm him down, but you could also run the risk of simply breaking off the negotiations or your relationship with him. Some confrontational personalities cannot tolerate the aggressiveness of others.

Kouatly – So, what should you do when confronted with an adversary who is consistently aggressive?

Phelizon – One of the most aggressive moves you can make is to hang up on someone. One day I was faced with such a situation. An extremely persistent businessman was very insistent on obtaining a favor from the company which I had no intention of granting. After I explained to him more than once that his request could not be satisfied, he got angry and hung up on me. I called him back immediately and said, "I don't know what happened. I think we must have been disconnected." He was silent for a moment, then started on a different topic that we were to discuss, in a tone that suddenly had become almost friendly.

Generally, though, I would say that in order to deal with an aggressive opponent, you must first start by understanding his motives. Perhaps he is aggressive because he does not want to negotiate, or because he just disapproves of doing business with you, or simply because he lacks experience and is afraid of being taken advantage of. So he starts by expressing his unreasonable demands, or makes brash statements like, "you can take it or leave it."

With someone like that, you must show that it's not by intimidating you that he will have the upper hand. You have to hold tight during his "tantrums" and on the contrary let go a little when you see him calm down. You must teach him the benefits of a trade-off and sometimes you must even accept losing a little so that he will want to repeat the experience.

In a formal setting, I think that against a very aggressive opponent, you must force yourself to speak in a calmer manner than him, ignore his threats, not respond to his outbursts, talk slower, not cut him off, and when he's finished with his diatribe, add to the dramatic climate even more by staying silent for a few seconds before responding. This attitude of "resistant conciliation" usually bears results.[3]

Kouatly – Is "resistant conciliation" a way of showing that you can make concessions without submitting?

Phelizon – Precisely. Submitting is accepting to be dependent. There is therefore a world of difference between concession and submission.

I remember a negotiation that took place under the most conciliatory terms in which neither party had accepted to submit to the other and where an agreement was very quickly reached.

In France, as you might know, some privately held companies inherited what has been called as "cross shareholding." That was the case for the company while I was CFO. Uncoupling these participations was not an easy job. But, it happened once at lightning speed. It was in 1997 and the president had agreed in principle to a buyout of about 200 million euros. All that needed to be done was to finalize the process. That was the task with which I was charged, in conjunction with my counterpart, a banker I knew well. Due to our calendars, and also for confidentiality, we agreed to meet on a Saturday morning. My counterpart had a number in mind, and I had another, but we were very close. We quickly decided to split the difference. We phoned our respective presidents who gave us their immediate approval. The "negotiation" hadn't lasted an hour.

This example of "speed negotiation" demonstrates that when both parties are ready to compromise, the endless discussions that usually precede all negotiations (and whose purpose sometimes is merely to tire the opponent) are needless. After all, *time is of the essence*, as the saying goes.

Kouatly – Anatoly, what do you think of this distinction between confrontational and conciliatory styles? I think that the British usually refer to "red" for confrontational and "blue" for concessionary. Does this distinction apply to chess players' styles?

Karpov – In the framework of a negotiation, the distinction is pertinent, but doesn't really apply to chess. When playing a match, you can't be just "conciliatory" or "confrontational." What happens is that you might be aggressive because your opponent annoys you, or decides to make a concession because you're tired.

Kouatly – During a match, it seems that often a player will exchange a piece for another. Wouldn't that characterize a concessionary style?

Karpov – For me, such moves don't indicate a style. Chess isn't about exchanging pieces, but taking them. Sure, sometimes you have to sacrifice one of your pieces to take another you judge more important, but this is because the setup of the game dictates it, not because you are more concessionary.

That's how you might sacrifice your bishop for a knight. Normally, you shouldn't do that because it's said that the bishop is worth more than the knight. But in some circumstances, it is the opposite, and the knight is in a much better position than the bishop. At the end of a game, for example, it is better to have a queen and a knight than a queen and a bishop.

The position of the pieces does have considerable importance and sometimes to win a position you must sacrifice important pieces. In that sense chess resembles a negotiation.

Kouatly – Let's look now at approaches. Jean-François, you said you distinguish three approaches. What are they?

Phelizon – The direct approach, the indirect approach, and the lateral approach.

The *direct* or *frontal* approach derives typically from martial or warlike behavior. This is the most immediate way to conduct your strategy. The goal is to make the enemy's forces surrender. Your plan takes no account of the *other* and consists of playing your all in a sort of double or nothing. "I engage the battle: heads I win—the opponent can only lay down his arms; tails I lose—I'm the one who has to lay down mine."

The *indirect* or *oblique* approach is more difficult to implement. The object is to use the opponent's forces by detouring them, even subverting them or taking advantage of its weaknesses (which amounts to the same thing). To be able to take the strengths and weaknesses of the *other* into account and use them to your advantage, you must not only know the ins and outs of his actions, but also be able to penetrate his strategic vision. That is why the indirect approach, though more efficient than the direct approach, is also less immediate.

The *lateral* approach is, without argument, the most subtle of the three. It is essentially suggestive and amounts to causing the opponent to act despite his intentions in a way which will in any event make him vulnerable. Therefore you should put him on the defensive by a stratagem, or make him negotiate before he even fights. This way he is led to change his own plan, or adopt a new plan different from the one he had prepared.

A business leader would take a direct approach when he says to one of his direct reports: "You are fired"; he would take an indirect approach when he says to one of his suppliers: "I would like to increase my business with you but you are much too expensive"; he would take a lateral approach when he says to the head of a company he wants to buy: "Don't engage a battle with me as I will buy your shares anyway."

Kouatly – Now let's look at each of the three approaches you cite. The most immediate, the direct approach, consists of using force. This is the one we will focus on in the following conversation.

Phelizon – Usually symbolizing the behavior of the strong toward the weak, the direct approach stems from impulse and seems to be the fastest way to fight a battle. La Fontaine illustrated this very well in the fable "The Wolf and the Lamb": *"The arguments of the strongest are always the best . . . "* "Might makes right."[4]

But a negotiation is different. When negotiating, the object is not to convince yourself of your own reasons, but to show the opposing party that it is in their interest to finalize a deal. Therefore, it is not good enough to make offers to your adversary; you must get him to accept them.

In the movie *The Fugitive*, there is a scene where Tommy Lee Jones, the FBI agent, has Harrison Ford backed up against a precipice. Harrison Ford is unjustly accused of murdering his wife and yells to the lawman, "You're wrong to want me dead. I am innocent." Jones replies that he doesn't care, and doesn't want to know if Harrison is guilty or innocent. His only job is to capture him. Just as at the negotiating table, it isn't important to know who's right or wrong. That's not the issue. The important thing is to end up cooperating.

Kouatly – Wasn't the direct approach inspired first by Rome?

Phelizon – Yes, the Romans perfected the art of the frontal attack, but we shouldn't forget the Greeks. In ancient Greece, phalanges consisted of an elite, heavily armed Hoplite corps, lined up one behind the other, advancing in tight formation, giving no opportunity to flee. The carnage resulting from the direct collision of two phalanges was actually an economic response: reduce the ravages of prolonged warfare to a winner-take-all duel, and by a brief and direct assault, reach a decision at once rapid and unequivocal.

Kouatly – In what way is the direct approach in essence confrontational?

Phelizon – It tends to *ignore* the opponent, whom you know nothing about and to whom you don't even want to speak. Let me also add that it doesn't take into account the time factor any more than the economic or psychological factors. That's why a frontal attack must be led quickly.

But, when you say speed, you are also saying cost. The direct approach is not particularly cheap. More precisely, it can only succeed under very specific circumstances, that is, when the forces at your disposition are clearly superior to those of the opponent (at least three times greater, say military tacticians), which is rarely the case. The combats of medieval knights, trench warfare, massive bombing, the search for a dominant economic position, and hostile takeovers all resort to direct approach.

Kouatly – So, the direct approach or "red" style—which is widely used since it is truly the essence of combat—is not an approach particularly useful in a negotiation, nor for that matter in a chess match.

Karpov – In chess, if two players are approximately of equal strength, the one adopting a style that is too confrontational would immediately give himself a heavy handicap. Obviously, it does happen that in simultaneous games, or when the players are mismatched, the strongest one might adopt a direct approach. But, in that case you cannot really call that a "game."

Phelizon – The "red" style is often a characteristic of someone with an inflated ego. But vanity is like a drug and the one whose pride is the most satisfied isn't usually the one who makes the best deal. This doesn't mean, however, that he cannot achieve his goals.

As an example, take someone who wants to buy something at any cost. He would barely listen to the seller and would merely say, "I have a lot of money; I'm in a hurry and I want your company. Name your price. Whatever it is, I accept." It may sound absurd but some recent acquisitions, even some large ones, seem to have followed this pattern. Of course, such an attitude on the buyer's part can certainly be considered arrogant. This behavior sometimes typifies the large corporation versus the small enterprise. Money is power and the other must submit. But if the small enterprise can play its hand correctly it can certainly make a great deal in the shadow of the large corporation. In the same way a large corporation can prosper in the shadow of a government.

But, when the power is about equal, pride rarely pays. I would therefore recommend that a negotiator banish the "me" in a discussion and use "we" (not the royal "we," but the true "we"). Rather than saying, "I have a problem with this point and I can't accept it," it would be better for him to say, "We have a problem here, let's try to resolve it together." After all, if there is a problem, it can only be resolved by dealing with the opposing party. In general, I would suggest to the negotiator that he listen carefully to what is being said, and indicate at regular intervals that he understands the message being delivered by repeating in his own words what he's just heard. This is how, with a little skill, he can discover his opponent's real motivations, which is the best way to insure the success of his mission.

Kouatly – Anatoly, you were saying a moment ago that the "red" or confrontational style was not recommended. There are, however, players who are very confrontational. What can you do then?

Karpov – One way to respond is by being extremely conciliatory, to disarm the opponent. That's what Tal[5] did when playing Botvinnik for the 1960 World Championships. Botvinnik was very meticulous and never left anything to chance. In his opinion, a chess match started long before the first game. When he began speaking with Tal about the organizational details for the world championship, Tal responded that he didn't want to discuss it and would accept all of Botvinnik's conditions: location of the match, number of games, etc. Tal was young. He probably wanted to show his opponent that he wasn't afraid of him and he could play under any conditions. He was a little like the buyer that Jean-François mentioned just now: "Tell me your terms and whatever your price, I will meet it."

Kouatly – Tal won that championship.

Karpov – Yes, but the following year, in 1961, he showed the same lack of concern and lost.

Kouatly – So the direct approach can only be used once because you can only take your opponent by surprise once?

Phelizon – "True, true, false," as the proverb goes.[6] Sometimes you can fool someone twice. Three times is much rarer. Usually, you don't negotiate the same way with people you will deal with in the future (union representatives, bankers, suppliers) and people you don't expect to see again (founders of a company who are selling to retire, for example). In the first instance, you must absolutely "leave something on the table" when you're done. In the second instance, it isn't necessary.

♟

HOW THE FOX ATE PINÇART THE HERON[7]

In the shade of a willow to his left, the fox saw Pinçart who was fishing. He immediately put his head down, lay flat, and wondered how to catch him.

What should I do? If I wait for him to come over to my side, I could wait a long time and then I might miss him. I must find a ruse. I can't stay here daydreaming forever with nothing to show for my time.

He tore up some of the reeds that covered the riverbank and threw them in the river. The reeds traveled down the stream toward the heron, who, seeing them, raised his head and jumped back. Realizing that it was just some reeds, he pushed them away with his beak and continued fishing.

Renard tore up another bunch and threw them also down the stream. The heron was frightened and jumped. But he came back toward the reeds, felt them with his foot and his beak, and scattered them. And seeing that again it was nothing but a bunch of reeds, he went back to fishing.

Renard, laying on the cool grass, his senses alert, had observed the heron's behavior. This time he ripped up a big bunch of reeds, packed them together, threw them in the water, and lay on top of them, covering himself with a few of the reeds in order to hide. Floating this way, he drifted toward the heron, who, preoccupied by fishing, wasn't on guard.

Pinçart saw the floating reeds coming toward him, but he felt no fear, thinking that it was just more reeds like the ones that had floated past him before. When Renard got close, baring his teeth, he jumped up, grabbed the heron by the neck, and dragged him under a hawthorn bush. With no concern for his cries, he strangled him. And when he had strangled him, he ate him.

Kouatly – You just said that when you decide to take the offensive, you break the dialogue with your opponent. But, sometimes you can speak to him in an abrupt, definitive manner.

Phelizon – That is what is known as the *ultimatum,* the last word, which is no more than a formal notice.

The vocabulary of the direct approach is usually *directive*, and is by definition very precise. As linguists say, it is extensive but not comprehensive. Without ambiguity, these words designate objects and processes with precision. A directive statement's purpose is to clearly highlight, to force, and to constrain. Therefore, the vocabulary of war is threatening and *closed*. As André Gluckman wrote, all battle plans exhaust the possible options. It is clear-cut.

Consequently, directive words have a strong operational connotation. The language of the CEO, the officer, the financial executive launching a hostile takeover is enforceable and coercive. To incite to action, an order must leave no room for interpretation. It is therefore peremptory and restrictive.

Note that the person using directive language wants to incite someone to action, but he doesn't always persuade. You can execute an order without approving of it.

Kouatly – What do you think of a negotiator who imposes a deadline to reach an agreement?

Phelizon – You must be very sure of yourself, not to say presumptuous, to impose a deadline in the course of a negotiation. I remember an anecdote that illustrates how wise a negotiator Nixon was. It was at the very end of the Vietnam War, during the discussions between the Americans and the North Vietnamese. "Kissinger was euphoric. He told Nixon that he intended to demand settlement before the November elections. But Nixon was very cautious. He thought if Kissinger included the election date in the negotiation calendar, that very fact would weaken his position vis-à-vis the North Vietnamese."[8]

In fact, in the "game" that is a negotiation, you must always be aware of two things: the first is not to paint yourself into a corner (for example when you advertise your objectives to the other party) and the second is not to make your adversary lose face. Especially if the opposing party reluctantly accepts a clause, you never should crow about it.

Kouatly – Is "conciliatory resistance" also effective with confrontational personalities who hide their game?

Phelizon – Yes, I think in that case you must always get back to the essence of a negotiation, which is an exchange (or more aptly a series of exchanges), and never consider giving something away for a song.

In a negotiation, you can never give something for nothing and you can never demand something at any cost. So, when you make a statement that expresses only what you want, you seek to get something for nothing and your attitude is aggressive. Not only will your counterpart not give you what you seek, but you will have weakened your position by revealing it.

Conversely, every time you make a statement where you give something away without getting anything in exchange, your attitude indicates submission. Not only will your opponent take for granted what you offer, but he will try to get even more at your expense.

Therefore, submission and aggression are both extreme behaviors and should be avoided at all costs. They are a little like chlorine and sodium, two deadly substances when ingested separately, but useful when combined in the form of table salt.

The counterpart to "conciliatory resistance," which is much more effective than submission, is "concealed aggression," which is much more effective than pure aggression.[9] Conciliatory personalities who resist and aggressive personalities who conceal really have a better chance of getting what they want than by showing their real nature.

The ideal, therefore, is to always manage to combine within the framework of conditional offers what you want to get with what you are willing to give. What a good negotiator says is, "If you give me what I want, I will give you what you want." He says it firmly, as to the principle of the condition, and very compromisingly when it comes to the nature of what he expresses. In a conditional offer, the "if" is not up for discussion, but the terms of the exchange must remain hypothetical and indicative.

ADAPTING TO CIRCUMSTANCES[10]

During the time of Springs and Autumns, Prince Wu of Zheng planned on some day annexing the Duchy of Hu. His military forces being limited however, he dared not attempt a frontal attack. To appease the Duke of Hu, who was very suspicious, Prince Wu offered him the hand of his most beautiful daughter. The Duke accepted and thus became his son-in-law.

A short time later, the Prince called his ministers together and said:

"I plan to attack a foreign nation. In your opinion which is the one most vulnerable?

One of the ministers answered that the obvious choice was the Duchy of Hu.

"What?" Exclaimed the Prince, pretending to be enraged. "How dare you propose that we attack the Duchy of Hu when the Duke has married my own daughter?"

And he immediately had the minister beheaded.

When the Duke heard the news, he could no longer doubt the sincerity of Prince Wu and felt that he no longer needed to exercise vigilance.

That's when Prince Wu launched a sudden attack against the Duchy of Hu. He took it over in the blink of an eye.

Kouatly – In the final analysis, even with the direct approach, everything is a matter of compromise. Each side must make offers to the other within the framework of their own "exchange logic," taking into account their remaining resources.

Phelizon – In the heat of the battle, however, you don't necessarily realize that you're exhausting your resources. Therefore, the first obligation of the negotiator, without question, is to conserve his bargaining chips.

Let's remember our physics class. To pass from a low orbit to a high orbit, an electron must acquire energy. Conversely, to go from a high orbit to a low orbit, it must release energy. The same applies to negotiations. When one of the parties looks for a compromise, scales back its demands, and declares itself ready for a concession, its change of position is often accompanied by an energy discharge that the other party needs to learn how to recognize and manage.

Karpov – I think that personal energy, that of the player or the negotiator, is often overestimated because fatigue comes on stronger after the action than during it. During the action, you function on nervous energy and you don't feel fatigue as acutely. But it is there sapping your resources.

Kouatly – How can your supply of energy be maintained at its peak during a match?

Karpov – That is a very important question and the answer varies from individual to individual. When you're facing the ordeal of a long match, you must have a plan in mind. Among other things, this plan must cover how you expect to manage your energy since your supply is not unlimited. All champions try to spread their energy consumption out in a balanced way during a tournament, so that they are not too weak in the beginning, stay strong throughout, and not exhausted at the end.

The problem is that you sometimes find yourself in difficult situations, with opportunities that you are not able to capitalize on and results that you don't anticipate. You might lose a game that you normally would have won because you took unnecessary risks. So, you get nervous and you use up a lot of energy. It's difficult to settle down: you are out of your comfort zone.

Chess players, when they face this kind of extreme tension, start experiencing real physical and psychological problems, just like negotiators working on nervous energy, trying to reach an unlikely agreement with the opposing party. They don't sleep as well. Sometimes, they don't sleep at all. In the worst case scenario, they "crack."

Of course, sometimes the temptation is to start taking medication, but frankly, I wouldn't advise doing that. Once in my life I took a sleeping pill. It was in 1978. I was playing Korchnoi. We were at the end of a tournament that had lasted 133 days. I was so exhausted the last two nights that I couldn't sleep. The doctor was with me and suggested that I take two sedatives. I swallowed only half of one and I did fall asleep. But the next day, I had a terrible headache, and even though I had slept at least eight hours, I really wasn't feeling well. I was obviously having trouble concentrating and that day was very difficult. So, after that less than satisfactory experience, I decided that I would never take any sleep medication again, even if I stayed up all night.

Later, completely by accident, I found a much more effective way to replenish my strength which I have often used since. I tried it out for the first time during my match with Anand, in 1998.[11]

It was at the end of the tournament. I only had a one-point lead by the second to last game. I was defending position quite well. Unfortunately, when I realized that this particular defense had given me back the advantage, my mind relaxed, I made a mistake and I lost the game.

But I still had two games to play. I was really feeling my loss and was having trouble sleeping. I got the idea to take a long shower, alternating the water temperature: very hot, then very cold, then very hot again, and so on. I immediately felt much better and was able to sleep. The next morning, I renewed the experience. I realized that this technique of taking a shower while alternating water temperatures managed to "perk" me up pretty well for a few hours.

Kouatly – It would seem to me that all demonstrations of strength also require speed. Isn't power the product of mass multiplied by speed?

Karpov – Speed is crucial in chess, as is mobility. Of course, you could win a "no pressure" game, if I may call it that, one in which you've prepared all the moves. You could even win a second game that way. But experience shows that preparing moves ahead of time is not a good way to win. Even if in theory you have the advantage, it's still a battle that takes place on the chessboard. Your advantage exists only if you are not a prisoner of what you had formulated in your mind. If you are not able to deviate from your plan, you run the risk of not being able to respond and if your adversary is aggressive, mobile, and quick, he will have every opportunity to defeat you. In any case, he will be the one leading the game.

Phelizon – It is clear that speed and strength are a winning combination. When you mount a frontal attack, you must have sufficient means. Insufficient means can cost you dearly. From that perspective, in order to be fully effective, a power move must be preceded by the concentration of all available forces.

But you can multiply the effect of concentrating your forces by swift execution. The direct approach therefore means concentration of forces *and* speed of execution, so that shock effect becomes the main factor.

Military men say that the concentration of forces is nothing without speed of execution. The philosopher Alain went even further saying that any method that seeks to conquer by speed is really a form of waging war. A business leader knows that even if he has accumulated financial means, "time is of the essence."

Kouatly – Isn't Kasparov a believer in the direct approach?

Karpov – I know Kasparov very well, and I can tell you that he has a very interesting personality. I have always greatly enjoyed talking with him, and even if during his career he beat me more often than

I beat him, I always felt that our games were about equal. Kasparov is very emotional. When we negotiated match conditions, he was only firm in front of a large audience. When I was beating him, I knew he was suffering. But in front of the press, the organizers, or anyone who wasn't a chess expert, he could play his part like an actor and pretend not to be affected.

In fact, Kasparov isn't an analytical thinker. He isn't really at ease when discussing specific points. But he hates his own vagueness. And, when he isn't sure, he becomes arrogant. He tried that with me two or three times, but when I snapped back that he could keep his arrogance for others, he calmed down quickly.

The arrogance Kasparov and some other players display is no longer in vogue. I think that since World War II, we in Europe and in the United States seem to no longer accept displays of power. The press, especially, loses interest in anyone who is overbearing and temperamental, even if he is a genius. The public interprets any kind of aggressive behavior as insulting and considers any aggressor as somebody unbalanced to say the least.

Kouatly – Would Kasparov be considered a "hidden aggressive" type?

Karpov – He always puts the pressure on, but sometimes bluffs. He tends to present himself as the obvious winner because he already knows everything. And if you haven't been warned, you could be impressed by a person who claims to never make a mistake.

As I said, Kasparov is an actor. He has crafted this personality for himself during his career and it seems to have worked for him. For a while, many grand masters did not want to play him because they were convinced of his superiority.

Phelizon – In the business world there are also flamboyant people who have forged the image of a winner for themselves. The press idolizes them, because, just like alchemists, they seem to transform the smallest endeavors into gold mines. Of course, it's not easy to post only successes, and often, the grandeur and extravagance of these tycoons hide mountains of debt that the best analysts haven't been able to or haven't wanted to uncover. So their fall is even more spectacular. I don't want to mention anybody in particular but we all have in mind some of these tycoons and how they display their *grandeur*.

Kouatly – Concentrating your forces somewhere means weakening your position elsewhere. From that perspective, is the direct approach the most risky?

Phelizon – Yes, I've said it before, there is a bit of an "all or nothing" aspect when you throw all your forces into a battle. If you win this way, you win more and faster. But, if you lose, you lose much more. All direct approaches are intrinsically risky, for any Goliath can meet his David. Power creates arrogance and arrogance always implies some form of weakness.

You must remember that any direct approach consists of engaging your forces without considering those of your opponent (meaning without knowing enough about them and mostly without taking advantage of them). It searches to resolve, by seemingly simple means and the shortest route, conflicts that you believe cannot be solved otherwise.

Kouatly – I get the impression that the use of direct approach often results from an overdeveloped ego.

Karpov – Some people have overdeveloped egos. I would add however that self-confidence in itself is not always a handicap. It can be an element of your inner strength. But when that confidence is excessive, it shows a weakness of character and that is important. As Jean-François was saying, vanity is like a drug. It keeps you from accepting even the smallest personal defeat.

Kouatly – Do you think that ego was one of the reasons why Fischer was reluctant to put his 1975 World Champion title back in play?

Karpov – Very possibly, I think.

Kouatly – What do you think of the direct approach? Are there circumstances where you would use it?

Karpov – I think it depends on how you feel and what your outlook is. If you live secluded from the world, you can afford that luxury. But, if you care about your reputation, your credibility, or if you are at the height of your career, it is probably best not to use the direct approach, even if you are stronger. There is an expression "Winners can't be wrong." The public, however, has no qualms about judging arrogant people.

Kouatly – As the Eastern proverb goes, "Better brief suffering than long pain."

Phelizon – Sainte-Beuve[12] also wrote, "You should never let your enemy feel the weak side, where with a little pressure, the sword can pierce." I don't think that the private equity firm, KKR, could ever have bought RJR Nabisco (this was a $26 billion[13] takeover) if they hadn't adopted a direct approach using massive fire power, involving impressive capital, and particularly fast action.

In the business world there are usually many advantages to being on the offensive. A company which is always the first to launch a product on the market can forge the reputation of being an innovative enterprise that others will have a hard time destroying. And experience has shown that companies that have been able to take the offensive before the others have often remained the leaders in their sector (3M comes to mind, for example).

Kouatly – And what are the drawbacks of a direct approach? Is this a "risk-taker's approach?"

Karpov – Obviously. It appeals more to "cowboys." In any case, it attracts those who like to plow straight ahead, without looking left or right. As we said, the direct approach assumes great fire power on the part of the attacker and requires two qualities that only a trained team can possess: precision and speed.

Phelizon – Anatoly is correct in saying that the direct approach is a "cowboy" approach. I would add that one of the drawbacks is that it consumes a lot of energy and resources.

Many losing and ill-planned operations can be cited, says the military strategist Sun Tzu in essence, but there are not many skillful ones that last long.[14] So, if you decide to adopt a direct approach, you must throw all your forces into the battle, go as fast as possible, and, obviously, not stop in the middle.

I would like to close this topic by citing Napoleon, one of the masters of the direct approach: "At the beginning of a campaign, you must think hard about whether to attack or not. But when the offensive has begun, you must sustain it until the very end; for, regardless of the loss of military honor, how deflated army morale will be, or the courage you give to the enemy, retreats are more disastrous and cost more in men and material than the bloodiest of engagements. The difference is that, in a battle, the enemy loses about evenly with you, whereas, in a retreat, you lose without him losing at all."[15]

CHAPTER 3

Indirect Approach: Strength against Strength

Take advantage of opponent's
weaknesses. – Tactical option of flight. –
Know when you can win. - Danger of
getting trapped. – "Pull when pushed,
push when pulled." – Protecting your
territory. – Take the path of least
expectation. – Suggestive language with
indirect approach. – Computers lack
intuition. – David can win over Goliath.

At the end of the game, the player who has the most territory points wins.
Rules for the game "Go."

Kouatly – In our last conversation, it was said that someone who engages in a frontal attack could be seen as oblivious of reality. Assuming he has prepared his attack, he knows the forces he's facing but a little like a boxer, he throws himself blindly at his opponent.

Another approach, probably smarter, can be one in which the strengths and weaknesses of the enemy are used against him. We will call this the indirect approach.

Phelizon – The indirect approach is usually indicated in a situation of strength against strength. A perfect illustration of this for me is the story of the Horaces and the Curiaces which took place during the reign of Tullus Hostilius, the third king of Rome.[1]

The cities of Rome and Alba were in constant conflict. One day, they agreed to what in the Middle Ages would be known as "the judgment of God." Romans and Albanians would pick champions who would do battle in the presence of the two armies. The city whose champions won would be declared the ruler of the other city.

Rome chose the three Horace brothers; Alba, the three Curiaces, and the battle began. On the first clash, two Horaces fell and all three Curiaces were injured. The surviving Horace, afraid that he would fall against his three combined adversaries, fled in order to split them up, convinced that they would follow at different speeds depending on the severity of their injuries. His plan proved correct. He turned suddenly, killed the Curiaces in succession, and assured Rome's triumph.[2]

What lesson can be drawn from this story? If the Curiaces had stayed together, they would have won. But through an error in judgment, they pursued at their own speed the surviving Horace and this direct action proved fatal.

The indirect action of the surviving Horace, however, gave him the victory.

Kouatly – In a negotiation, how can you use the opponent's strengths to your advantage—or take advantage of his weaknesses?

Phelizon – Let me just use a personal example. Once, I had to deal with a very arrogant buyer. For its own reasons, a group wanted to buy one of our affiliates over time, at a very attractive price for us. They spoke of 500 million euros, 150 more than the next closest offer we received. But we had limited confidence in the financial capabilities of this group and after a few negotiating sessions I demanded a bank guarantee for the amount that would be due to us after the agreement of sale was signed.

The lead negotiator was very offended. He asked me in essence why I didn't trust him. He offered all kinds of references, and loudly stated that he, too, could demand guarantees. He then enumerated a list of issues on which he could have doubts. "How do I know that your books are accurate? That your inventory is up to date? That you have sufficient funds?" Of course, I stood my ground. The group I work for doesn't have the reputation of embellishing the books.

Then, all of a sudden, angry and flushed, he yelled, "Your stubbornness towards me is absolutely uncalled for. Since you have decided to act in this disrespectful way towards me, I am breaking off negotiations." And, furious, he left the meeting with his team.

I was upset, but what was I supposed to do? All that we could do was go home. But, the exit that we had witnessed just reinforced our opinion that a bank guarantee was an absolute prerequisite for this deal.

It turned out that it was only a false exit, or I should say a bad move. A few days later, through a third-party attorney, the buyer knocked on our door and we resumed our discussions. Of course his grand exit put him in a very vulnerable position; now we knew how badly he wanted to do this deal. I took advantage of this by demanding a guarantee from a top-ranked bank and a few other things, which he could no longer refuse.

Kouatly – The legend of the Horaces and Curiaces illustrates well the effectiveness of fleeing, the height of indirect action. Flight is a tactic recommended by many strategists.

Phelizon – The thirty-sixth stratagem does recommend flight when in a situation that is all but lost.[3] Chinese military authors thought that in war, going forward should seem as natural as going backward. Consequently, when you do not wish to engage in battle, you must know how to give some ground. By avoiding a complete defeat, you have a better chance of ultimately being victorious.

Karpov – I think that flight is always a tactical option that deserves consideration. But it comes with an "if." You must control the situation. Some players make strange decisions, play a bizarre game, open all doors, but have no idea where they're going. They are constant losers because they do not control the situation.

Not too long ago, Spassky confided to me of an instance when he was considering competing for the world championship (it was in the 1960s and he was still young), he felt able to master any situation on a chessboard, even under the most difficult circumstances.

Then he became world champion, wrote a book analyzing his various games, and started getting a little older.[4] At the age of forty-five, he realized he wasn't always able to control what was happening on the chessboard. That's normal. When you're young and full of energy, you can easily play a game with full attention from beginning to end. Even if you lose, you understand fully why. But, with age, you find it difficult to sustain your attention at peak level for long hours. Your mental activity is up and down. You're clear and focused for a while, then you relax a little, then you're focused again, and so on.

Therefore, controlling the situation is always difficult. When they're young, the best players want to be in control of everything, all the time, with every move they make. But they realize that doing that is almost impossible. With time they learn to control the situation at crucial moments even if they are less attentive when everything is going "as usual."

Kouatly – In tennis, they say that a champion is the one who finds in himself sufficient resources to serve aces when he's in trouble.

Karpov – That is a constant in all battles. When in combat, regardless of the kind, you may find yourself in very diverse situations. First, you need to start the fight concentrating on details, just to test your strength or your adversary's reactions. This phase is very important for it enables you to prepare mentally for the upcoming events. If, after the first skirmishes, you are convinced you have a handicap and you're going to lose, don't take it too seriously. You can't always win. Try rather to understand the reasons for your probable defeat. You will accept it more easily and, revitalized, will soon be able to get your revenge.

 If, to the contrary, you are firmly convinced that you can win, then marshal all your resources and energy. Victory will enhance your mental strength and comfort you with the idea that you are stronger than your opponent. But if you know that you can lose, you run the risk of experiencing a devastating psychological shock.

 That's how I have proceeded throughout my career. First, I take stock as clearly as possible of the forces present. Then I accept that I might lose. Mostly, I fight like a lion, without ever relaxing, when I know I can win.

Kouatly – You have the reputation of being an uncompromising player.

Karpov – Yes, I think I've always been considered a "tough" player. Why? Because when I've decided to fight for a prize I think is worth it, I will do everything, absolutely everything I can to win. Nothing will make me give up and everyone knows it.

Kouatly – What happens when both sides adopt an indirect approach?

Karpov – Then there is a good chance that nothing will go the way you want.

 That's what happened in 1978 when Korchnoi and I had to determine where the next world championship would take place. At that time, interested countries had to present their proposals to the FIDE (World Chess Federation). The FIDE would then formally inform the two players of the options and the players would then indicate their preferences. Classification was very simple: 1 for the country they preferred, 2 for their next choice, and so on. The country that won was the one with the lowest score.

I remember that seven countries were in the running. Three of them—France, Italy, and a third I forget—weren't very serious about the prize money they were offering the winner. The four other competing countries were Austria, Germany, the Netherlands, and the Philippines. I didn't want to play in the Netherlands or in Austria because their national federations were too close to Korchnoi. And, just as in 1975 when it was Fischer's choice, neither did I want the Philippines. I knew that Korchnoi did not want the Philippines either. My preference was Germany, for at that time I was very tied to the German Chess Federation. Therefore, I placed Germany in first place, a blank in second position, and the Philippines in third. Korchnoi, for his part, naturally put Austria in first place, the Netherlands in second, and the Philippines in third. When Campomanes, the president of the FIDE, opened our response forms, he noticed that the only country we had both mentioned was the Philippines, a country that in reality neither of us wanted. So, he decided that the championships would take place in Manila.

Kouatly – So, you both lost.

Karpov – Yes. And then we started some indirect maneuvering where we found ourselves trapped again.

Through third-party negotiators, Korchnoi and I started thinking about how we could change this choice that satisfied neither one of us. Representatives from the Austrian and German federation got together and offered a new joint proposal. The match would take place half in Austria and half in Germany. In addition, the prize money would increase from $750,000 to $1 million.

The president of the German Federation called me to tell me that Korchnoi agreed to say that he would claim responsibility for the new proposal, but that he did not want to be the one to transmit it to the FIDE. So, I wrote to the FIDE saying that the Austrian/German proposal backed by Korchnoi was now my first choice. But then Korchnoi made a mistake. Without paying attention, he wrote a letter to the FIDE saying that this proposal initiated by me had his support.

When the president of the FIDE compared our two letters, he wasn't happy at all. "What is this? Which one of you took the initiative to change my decision? This is a setup!" Before we could even react, he contacted President Marcos, who publicly assured him of his support, and he let us know that in any case it was too late now to make any changes.

And that's how we both got trapped.

Kouatly – The indirect approach is obviously harder to implement than the direct approach.

Phelizon – Yes, naturally, because its aim is to use the adversary's forces by turning them, even subverting them, or—and this amounts to the same thing—taking advantage of his weaknesses. But to be able to gauge the strengths or weaknesses of the opponent, you must know not only the details of his actions, but also penetrate this strategic vision. In addition, indirect action *also* means circumventing the opponent's will. At the very least, it supposes that you've *considered* his plan, because yours will be exercised in relation to it, whereas in direct action your plan is exercised independently of the adversary's reactions.

That is the reason this approach, even though more efficient than the direct approach, is also less immediate. It cannot be adopted without taking into consideration the time factor, or your opponent's probable reactions, or even some psychological factors. Just like direct action, it derives from impulses, but its true motivator is the impulses of the *other party*.

Kouatly – Isn't the indirect approach inspired by the Japanese?

Phelizon – Even though most of the Japanese martial arts schools are founded on an indirect approach when confronting an opponent, many other sources of inspiration can be found. Aside from the example of the Horaces and Curiaces that I cited earlier, the combat between David and Goliath or the conquest of Mexico by Hernán Cortés are famous examples of the indirect approach. Similarly, public offerings that are only successful when the financial resources of the target company can be used typically constitute an indirect frontal approach. It is a skillful way to increase the financial means at your disposal. You simply dip into the treasury of the target company by securing the loan up front. That is what the financial engineers do. Such a process is related to indirect action since it consists of using the adversary's resources to your advantage.

But, it is true that the indirect approach is essentially of Japanese inspiration. In Japan, the masters of *bujutsu*[5] have always considered that the fundamental principles of martial arts should be applied to take advantage of the idiosyncrasies of the opponent. More precisely, by the principle known as *unilateral*, the opponent is the main target of the attack or the counterattack and the goal is to defeat him. In the principle known as *bilateral*, he is not only a target, but also an instrument. Many possibilities have resulted which have considerably enriched the art and culture of combat.

Hence, *jiû-jitsu* (literally the *art of flexibility*) is founded on the opposition of gentleness and force (or elasticity and stiffness). It recommends keeping the body full of *ki*, meaning psychic energy, maintaining your limbs as supple as possible, and staying always alert. There will come a time when, by consuming the least of your own energy possible, you will be able to use the adversary's strength against him.

These two principles of unilateral and bilateral action were used not only in individual combat. They were also often applied to large-scope military operations by Japanese generals from medieval times through World War II.

Kouatly – In judo classes you're taught to "pull when you're pushed" and "push when you're pulled."

Phelizon – Professor Kano, the inventor of judo,[6] used to often say, "You must pull when pushed, and push when pulled." In the first case, when your opponent launches an attack by using his strength against you, you must try to "bend" this force by deflecting it, and dissipating its effects, before counterattacking. Your opponent then will be practically deprived of reaction since he has just discharged his energy against you. In the second case, when your opponent tries to draw you to him, you can achieve the same "bending," deflecting, and dissipating effects. All you need to do is go with the movement instead of resisting it. Correctly done, this maneuver will contribute to destabilizing your adversary.

In Aïkido schools, the principle of indirect action is a little different.[7] It can be expressed this way: "Turn when you are pushed and enter when you are pulled." In the first case, an attack is neutralized by creating a kind of centrifugal force around you that forces your adversary to deflect his power from the center to the periphery. In the second case, the power that is pulling you is neutralized by aiming for your opponent's center. This creates an imbalance between the forces and improves conditions for a counterattack.

The difference between the principles of judo and Aïkido is subtle. In both instances, you use the opponent's power—pushed to the extreme it could mean his strategies, even his ideas—to reinforce your own strength. Noteworthy in these principles is the underlying concept of adaptability. For, if you want to use the opponent's power, you must obviously adapt your methods and behavior to his. Asians use the expression "riding the tiger"[8] to symbolize this behavior.

Karpov – How the application of the "pull when you are pushed" and "push when you are pulled" principles applies to chess is an interesting question that needs some thought. In chess history, there are famous battles that I think proceed from this principle. I'm reminded in particular of certain games between Tal and Korchnoi. Tal loved combinations and played a very offensive game. He could sacrifice pieces easily. Korchnoi was exactly the opposite. He often took what we call "poison pawns." And he could stay on the defensive for a very long time and reverse the situation at the very last minute.

Kouatly – Actually Tal and Korchnoi had such opposing styles that they seemed to almost dictate their approach.

Karpov – The games that Tal and Korchnoi played were always interesting because they always fought without subterfuge, one constantly sacrificing pieces and the other taking them. Actually Tal was always the attacker, Korchnoi the defender, a little like Petrosian. One believed in his intuition and preferred the direct approach; the other waited for a mistake to be made to react and preferred the indirect approach. They complemented each other.

That being said, they were somewhat prisoners of their style, and didn't really concern themselves with what was going on in their opponent's mind, because they were convinced that their plan was best. All the moves were well oiled. Tal said, "I attack." Korchnoi answered, "Go ahead, I'm waiting. My defense is in place. Regardless of what you do I will be able to repel your attack." Tal would then continue, "You want to play defense? OK. You won't be able to resist." And on and on. It was almost a dance. That's why Tal was always happy to attack Korchnoi's king (although he didn't like Korchnoi attacking his). But Korchnoi was happy with Tal's attack on his king, because he was convinced that Tal would lose against his defense.

Of course, the behavior of these two players was a bit of a caricature. Usually, players are supposed to think about the "why" of their opponent's moves, especially at the beginning of a game when most of the variables are known.

A player is often asked why he takes so much time in thought at the beginning of a game when precisely all the variables are well known. It's not that he's afraid of forgetting something, it's that he has to remember all the theory, try to determine what his opponent is thinking, and keep some element of surprise. If you wish, he has to figure out how he will be able to "pull when he's pushed" or "push when he's pulled."

You'll notice that these situations are exactly opposite but entirely complementary. So you can go from one to the other with relative ease. If, for example, you think your position is too vulnerable, you can be tempted to abandon the approach you had chosen, direct or indirect. By doing this, you would have to totally modify your plan, and therefore change the way you had been playing the game up until then. There is a strong possibility of going from defense to offense or vice versa, which is part of judo, or Aïkido principles.

Kouatly – When should you adopt an indirect approach? Should the power ratio be about one to one?

Phelizon – Yes, that's about right. If you are definitely stronger than your opponent, you can use a direct approach.

If you are as strong as him, the indirect approach makes the difference, since you actually deflect a portion of the opponent's strength to your advantage.

But, as we will see further on, if you are definitely weaker than the opponent, neither of these approaches is feasible. To have any chance of winning, you will need to be more subtle.

For instance, suppose that you want to buy a company. If you have all the financial means that you need, you will just buy it. If you are just about having the money to buy it, you can refine your business plan by using the treasury of your target to add to your financial means. If you are definitely poorer or weaker than your target, it is probably difficult for you to envisage buying it except if you can convince their Board that there is a very good reason for you and them to consider, say, a merger.

Kouatly – In the game of Go, you also use the strengths and weaknesses of the opponent.

RULES FOR THE GAME OF GO[9]

- The game is played on a checkerboard (*gô-ban*) made up of 19 vertical lines and 19 horizontal lines.
- The two players have 181 black stones and 180 white stones for a total of 361 stones for 361 intersections.
- The stones are placed alternatively by each player on any square of the *gô-ban*, including the borders. All have the same value and are static and immobile, except when captured and removed from the game.
- Any stone completely encircled by the opponent is taken prisoner and retired from the *gô-ban*. The same applies to any group of adjacent stones.
- The object of the game is to surround as many open intersections (territories) with your stones as possible, while losing the least possible (a stone captured from the enemy equals an intersection and vice versa).
- At the end of the game the player who has the most territory points wins.

Karpov – Yes. *Go* players use black and white tokens on a board. The game consists not only of creating but also of protecting a territory as vast as possible. In order to accomplish that, it is imperative to concentrate on the decisive battle(s), at the risk of weakening yourself in the secondary zones, therefore accepting partial defeats. The game of *Go* illustrates well the idea that the main purpose of a strategy is not just to win the battle but the entire war.

This surrounding tactic is also applicable to chess, but with a nuance. In chess, we say that when a piece has been locked in for a long time, it can surge out with incredible strength once released.

Kouatly – Isn't letting the opponent dig in also part of the indirect approach?

Phelizon – Yes, if the opponent digs in to a specific position, he weakens himself, and therefore you can take the advantage. That is the other aspect of the indirect approach, which consists not only of taking advantage of your opponent's strengths but also of his weaknesses.

Classical Chinese literature has often opposed the concepts of "empty" and "full." Over and over it is repeated that in order to be victorious, you must know how to advance on the "empty" parts of the enemy (meaning his weaknesses) and stop when you find his "full" parts (meaning his strong points).[10]

Kouatly – We've stressed that the element of surprise greatly increases the effect of a direct approach. How does it affect the indirect approach? Is it as important to surprise the opponent?

Phelizon – In his *World History of Strategy*, the English historian Liddell Hart writes that in effect, if a move made around the enemy front and directed against his rear amounts to following the path of least resistance, its equivalent in the psychological domain is the action least expected, or path of least expectation.[11] The relationship between these two concepts is evident. In order to produce its full effect, an attack on the "empty areas" must be unexpected.

Kouatly – So, rather than putting into play forces that confront each other straight on, an indirect action works on the levers that operate the opponent's forces. Jean-François, you've told us that the type of language that corresponds to direct action is directive. What would you call the one that applies to indirect action?

Phelizon – That would be *suggestive*. In this type of language, the object is less to dictate to the other than to take advantage of his arguments. The one talking tries to stay inscrutable, veiled, therefore revealing nothing of objectives. This kind of language actually stems from uncertainty. By always leaving something more to be said, alternating moments when the hint is clearer with those when it is more disguised, it enables the speaker to advance by stages. It makes it easier to get the other to accept, to make him *understand*. When you use the suggestive mode, the art consists less of convincing the other by speaking to his reason than to make his will wobble, which is to say weaken his resolve. In this, we clearly see the principles of the indirect approach. Suggestive language is the perfect complement to directive language. Direct language brings things brutally to light. It forces. It commands. Indirect language, on the contrary, gives the impression that the more transparent, the more redundant it seems, the more it may contain hidden meaning. In other words, the less it says, the more it hints.

THE OBLIQUE APPROACH[12]

The oblique approach allows both the one criticizing and the one arguing to stay covered and inscrutable while at the same time giving unlimited attack power. By always having more to say, since it alternates moments where the hint is more direct with moments when it becomes more veiled, criticism contains within itself the principle of unending oscillation. From a strategic point of view, the oblique approach translates into implicit language. The indirectness of the path leads to depth of meaning.

For Chinese writers, directive language was used to expose things without having to censure themselves. Suggestive language was used to express things without daring to be too direct, as if afraid. This way, they could make a sort of oblique language correspond to a sort of oblique action recommended by strategists.

To summarize, sometimes you should be able to say: "You will launch the attack tomorrow at 5 AM" or "you have six months to reduce your overhead by 20 percent"; sometimes it is better to say: "Your honor and your reputation are in play in this offensive" or "If I were you, I would launch a project aiming to reduce drastically the overhead."

Kouatly – In chess, games played against computers are often won using the principles of indirect action. But, is playing against a computer still playing chess?

Karpov – Certainly, no question about it, but it's a different game. I was always against the idea of opposing players to computers in tournaments. But, as far as matches are concerned, I have no objection. Tournaments are different. Why? Because the techniques required are very specific. There are ways to play against computers. Some players are comfortable with them, others not at all.

Kouatly – I guess they find this type of conflict disconcerting.

Karpov – In the beginning, the programs were easily circumvented. But they've been refined and their calculating power in particular has exploded. Today, when you are up against a computer, you cannot afford to take any chances. You must continue to perform detailed analyses of the situation. Therefore, you cannot sacrifice a single piece, you cannot try to innovate and you must try to keep the game going as long as possible. Since current computers are capable of doing millions and millions of operations per second, you cannot hope to beat them in that area. You would waste your time and energy for nothing. A computer calculates with ease (I would say that's all it does), but your brain is built differently. You must continually test your analysis, verify that you haven't made a mistake, and since your energy is limited (unlike the one supplying the machine across from you), you naturally have a handicap.

What computers lack are intuition and experience. Of course, they can dig into databases, but a database is not the same as years and years of accumulated experience. This is especially important at the end of a game when tested experience is required to know how to choose the pieces you want to keep. That's how you decide to finish the game with bishops, or knights, or a knight and a rook, when there are many more pieces on the board that you are getting ready to exchange. I think in that area players are much better than computers.

To play without taking any risks during the game and only start taking control at the end relates to the indirect approach in the sense that computers only reveal their weaknesses at the end of the game.

A POSITIONAL GAME LESSON[13]

While awaiting the victory of the IBM team, Kasparov, running low on time, checks the clock before throwing the engineer across from him one of the famous killer looks that are his trade secret and have deflated the morale of more than one flesh and blood player. These brief moments of rebellion are followed by a sort of dejection. Slumped in his armchair, stiff in his three-piece suit, his complexion gray, he appears to be looking for help, his eyes vague. His Maginot line is taking water. As desperate as it is, his resistance seems no longer effective. He knows he won't prevail. Deep within his defense the queen and rook of Deeper Blue twirl dangerously around him. Garry Kasparov, the king in desperate straits, is mercilessly attacked. The vein on his forehead pulses. In a flash, he shakes the engineer's hand, signs his slip, gets up, and leaves the camera's field. A few flights down, the public applauds raucously and gives the IBM team a standing ovation.

Kouatly – You describe the situation today, but software continues to progress. What will it be like tomorrow?

Karpov – I'm not convinced that software can be significantly improved. It would be real progress if computers could be self-teaching. For example, if they could never make the same mistake twice. That was Botvinnik's idea when he started to work on a chess software program.

He always said that using computers just to calculate was a waste. Obviously it represented enormous technological progress, but it didn't enable the programmer to imitate a player's brain. So, Botvinnik created the basics for an auto-teaching program, but he didn't get very far.

It is true that software continues to make progress to the extent that computers go a little faster every year. But the programs are always built the same way. They calculate, and calculate, but don't learn. Computers will improve the depth of their calculations, but the ramifications of possibilities are so extensive and exponential that even machines that are ten times more powerful than today won't be able to make a significant difference. In any case, they will never be able to "resolve" a game from beginning to end. Even supposing that the person programming the chess software is a very great champion himself (which is rarely the case), he would still have to be able to transfer his intuition and experience to the machine for the program to replace man. How do you do that? How do you teach something like that to a machine?

I did say though that some players enjoy playing against computers and others hate it. Actually those who hate it often just lose their nerve. What they don't like is to have "someone" across from them who is in complete control of themselves, entirely confident. They become obsessed wondering if they really did make the right move or if they made a mistake. They focus on the fact that they can't make even the slightest mistake during at least four fifths of the game and that's what makes them nervous.

Phelizon – When you read in the news that a player is pitted against a machine, it isn't quite the truth. In fact, as Anatoly has said, he is playing against a programmer who has "gelled" calculations and processes through his software. This is why the fight is indirect: the player is indirecly fighting against the programmer. Now, what makes the game uneven is that the programmer has all the time he wants to write the program whereas the player is constrained by the match's time limitations. Furthermore, it is extremely rare that these software programs are available to the public. They remain black boxes that the players can't examine.

IMPLICIT AND EXPLICIT ELIMINATIONS[14]

Often, a grand master has intuition. He thinks differently than a novice, or more precisely, his references are different. It is always a surprise to see that in a match, a grand master doesn't necessarily use a higher level of analytical thinking than a beginner. Truth be told, a grand master only considers a small number of moves. But the way he looks at the chessboard functions like a filter. He doesn't "see" bad moves when evaluating a situation. A beginner blocks out only the illegal moves. He has structured his perception of the game in such a way that he would never consider moving a rook diagonally or a bishop in a straight line. The grand master has also structured his perception of the board. But for him, bad moves are just as invisible as illegal moves are to most players. You could call that an *implicit* elimination of some of the branches of the tree of possibilities. In opposition to that, an *explicit* elimination of these branches would imply considering all possible moves and after analysis, deciding or not to take them into consideration.

That being said, as powerful as it may be, a computer is nothing more than a calculating machine. It only appears "intelligent." This is especially clear when working on form recognition (or automatic translation). The human mind can interpret an imperfect picture or understand an incomplete message. Anyone can understand a telegram wishing you "est ishes for appiness" or a wine list offering "Mondav Opu One." But, imperfections surprise most programs. Machines don't know how to treat semantic reductions. That is why they cannot compare to the human mind.

Kouatly – So, chess programs that can rival a world champion are not for anytime soon.

Karpov – Today, the best programs are grand master level, no more.

But, I would like to come back to what Jean-François was saying about the imbalance between a player and a software program. Today computers can access extremely large databases, and they dispose of unimaginable volumes of information. They know every game a player at a certain level has waged throughout his career. Players have a certain knowledge of chess history, but they cannot memorize everything in the databases. Therefore, they have a serious handicap.

On the other hand, computers have specific basics for openings and endings. But most computers don't "play" endings. They just estimate the final position. They calculate that such a position will win the game in 25 moves, another in 21, and yet another in 27. So, the program doesn't think. When its opponent moves a piece, the computer, after performing all its calculations, simply says, "Ah! If I do this, I am only 24 moves from victory." By doing this, it always plays the same way. It never forgets anything, but it doesn't invent anything either. . . .

To make matches interesting, programmers would have to agree to communicate their databases, making them available to both players, man and machine. This brings me back to what I was saying: if this were to happen, unless the programmer himself is a champion, I believe that the machine would clearly show its inferiority.

Phelizon – In any case the matches would be more interesting. All the psychological dimensions of a battle would be present. Instead of testing the player on the limits of his resistance (which is what happens today), there would be a real duel between player and programmer.

Kouatly – It seems that the appearance of information technology in the back offices has changed the cards. It seems it should reduce uncertainty. But doesn't it minimize a player's influence, even negate certain elements of surprise?

Karpov – Because of microcomputers, there is a big difference between the chess played in the 1970s and what is played today.

When you analyze a game, very often you feel the need to refer to something you've read. You know it's probably such and such page from such and such book, but you don't remember the exact content of the page. Back then, in order to be sure to find the correct reference, you had to have enormous documentation. There were always a number of people on the team who did research in the literature, even though it was time-consuming. I remember a match with Korchnoi where we brought cases and cases of books on chess—almost a ton. Among the books there was even an old one by Capablanca dating from 1934 that I had brought along, because it contained a lot of ideas and useful commentary.

Nowadays, all the literature fits on a microcomputer or at least on a few CD-ROMS. There are very powerful search programs that enable you to quickly find what you want. You can't use them during a game because games are not always adjourned, but the microcomputer is an incomparable analysis tool when you are preparing.

Kouatly – What happens when one player adopts the direct approach and the other the indirect approach?

Phelizon – I would say that the Davids often win over the Goliaths.

Karpov – Or the judo practitioner usually holds more trump cards than the boxer.

CHAPTER 4

Lateral Approach: Playing with Finesse

No point in struggling. –
Psychologically disarm the
opponent. – Creating new solutions.
– Finesse vs. trickery. – Using
stratagem to win. – Determine the
breaking point. – Lateral approach
popular in economic world. –
Stratagems at the negotiating table.
– Approaches of Tallyrand, Kissinger,
Gromyko. – No leaks. – Thorough
analysis. – Prior preparation. –
Convince opponent to stop fighting.

Psychological handicaps are sometimes enough to decide the outcome of a battle between two protagonists.
Paul Keres

Kouatly – All athletes know that competitions are won in the mind. Rather than pitting physical strength against physical strength, there is a third approach that Jean-François calls lateral, which favors the psychological factors inherent to all confrontations, or as the military say, morale.

Phelizon – That is obviously the most subtle approach, since, pushed to its extreme, it consists of convincing the opponent that there is no point in struggling, as he will without a doubt lose. Of course, everything is in the "without a doubt." When you are sure you are going to lose, a negotiated surrender seems better that an unconditional capitulation.

Kouatly – Doesn't morale have to be at its lowest point to even consider surrendering without a fight?

Phelizon – Of course, but this situation happens more often than you think because it results from an objective analysis of strengths.

Kouatly – Why is that?

Phelizon – I would like to refer again to the classical Chinese authors who recommend doing everything possible to avoid direct confrontation with the enemy army. For them, a frontal attack, where both armies proceed head on, is always risky and destructive. The art of warfare consists, on the contrary, of depriving the adversary of his defenses, sapping them from the inside, before any engagement even takes place so that he crumbles on his own, his morale deflated. Sun Tzu wrote, "The wise general is not the one who wins 100 victories in 100 battles, but the one who wins without fighting."[1]

Since unnecessary and lengthy military operations are always costly in both men and resources, it is by using this potential cost that you might convince an adversary to surrender without fighting. It is however better to address the very reasons for his hostility. That's why Sun Tzu recommends first attacking the enemy's plans and his strategy, then his alliances, his troops, and only then his strongholds. The most successful general, he adds, is the one you don't even think of praising, since he defeats an enemy who is defeated in advance.[2]

Therefore, if the lateral approach is usually the best approach, it is because it best demonstrates the principle of economy of strength.

Kouatly – Using this as our premise, the next question is obviously "how." How can you convince the opponent that he will be "surely" beaten?

Phelizon – Perhaps simply by words. As in the typical story of the fox of the fable, who manages to outsmart the crow without striking a blow. What does the fox want? He wants the piece of cheese that the crow, perched in a tree, is holding in his beak. The fox cannot adopt a frontal approach for fear the crow will fly away. So, he starts flattering him and praising his beautiful song (no matter if what he says is true or not). Thanks to this ruse, with this lateral approach, the crow begins to sing and lets go of the cheese which the fox snatches away.[3]

In the end, the fox defeats his opponent with his words. He submits him to his ways without combat, which, as Sun Tzu believes, is the ideal.

Karpov – In chess, convincing an adversary that he is beaten from the start is not an easy task. I'm talking about very high-level champions, of course. Journalists often ask if there is some kind of psychological preparation to strengthen your self-control. The answer is no, except for rare instances. When it comes to technique, however, you arrive in top form. Players who have won difficult contests are not easily intimidated.

That being said, for this small number of players who make up the elite at the world level, it is interesting to watch how a match unfolds on the psychological level. From the start, each protagonist is confident he can win. Just look at the famous games between Spassky and Fischer, or some of my games against Korchnoi or Kasparov. Consider in particular the famous world championship between Capablanca and Alekhine.[4] It was a very long match that lasted thirty-six games (the winner was the first one to score six victories). Capablanca kept saying that he would win and he was born to stay world champion until he died. Alekhine, for his part, didn't think for a moment that Capablanca could beat him. Each was completely sure of himself and convinced of his talent.

Kouatly – But "the art of war is the art of deceiving."

Phelizon – Yes, that's true. Long before Mahomet, Sun Tzu had said it.[5]

Karpov – And that's when the psychological aspect comes into play between two uncontested champions.

In my case, after two or three games, I have a pretty good idea of how an opponent I know feels about his positioning and what his intentions are. His game is almost an open book for me and I know how to influence him, even deceive him. I would guess that in the business world, the same thing happens.

When you know the other party well, you probably have a good idea what his intentions are. The arena is probably very much like a chess championship. The best lawyers and the best bankers assist veteran businesspeople. Both sides are usually talented and convinced that they will end up signing an agreement that benefits them. Neither one is ready to give up in advance. Obviously, that doesn't mean they won't start maneuvering to psychologically disarm the opposing team.

Phelizon – Since a negotiation consists of finding a compromise, the final agreement reached is never considered ideal by the two opposing parties at the beginning. Both must give in a little. But, at some point during the discussions, perhaps you say, "I can accept what's being offered. I could try to get more, naturally, but maybe it's best if I stop now before he changes his mind." That's one way of "surrendering." When you find yourself in that situation, everything happens as if—your opponent having used sufficiently convincing arguments—you feel that it would be useless to continue the duel since you have achieved the main objective you had set for yourself.

The goal of a negotiation is to agree on the exchanges. You are always free to accept the terms or not. In chess, the situation is more complex because the players are not seeking to reach agreement on a compromise. They can play the cat and mouse game as well.

Kouatly – But negotiators sometimes reach an agreement very quickly.

Phelizon – In very rare instances, both opponents reach a mutually satisfactory "happy medium" very quickly. I say in "rare instances" because this kind of agreement is largely based on trust, or on information that both parties agree to share. In that case, the protagonists are a bit like poker players who would put all their cards on the table right up front.

I think only once in my life was I able to reach this "happy medium" very quickly. We were in discussions to acquire a large enterprise whose majority shareholder was a bank. This bank needed cash, but because the tax bureau had granted it special tax benefits, it couldn't sell the majority of its holdings before a specific date which was relatively far into the future. On our side, we didn't want to purchase a minority. We wanted to have control of the company from the very first day and consolidate the totality of their figures into our accounts.

After numerous discussions, together we came up with the following solution: we agreed to purchase a minority share on the day we signed the contract, with the remainder of the shares two years later. On his end, the seller agreed to vote with us at Board and Shareholder meetings as soon as the contract was signed. Having thus control of the company from day one, our accountants authorized us to consolidate our participation by total integration into our accounts. And since he had only sold a minority of his shares, the seller continued to take advantage of the special tax benefits. He paid taxes on the profit only, at a reduced rate, when we made the second payment.

Karpov – You are right to emphasize that this story is not the norm. If both parties put all their cards on the table before even starting discussions, no battle would ever take place, and no deal could be made. A confrontation would theoretically be impossible. Of course you can make overtures during a battle or be frank during a negotiation, if only to show goodwill. But not all can be disclosed. Your opponent cannot know everything. You must keep some secrets to yourself.

Kouatly – In the fable from La Fontaine, the fox appears to be what he is: a sly operator. But are deceit, trickery, and cunning desirable traits?

Phelizon – The lateral approach stems from the usual behavior of the *strong over the weak*. "Need, the doctor of stratagem," La Fontaine wrote somewhere.[6]

The notion of stratagem is not just of Chinese[7] inspiration, it is also Greek, Arab, and Russian. The Greeks used the word *mètis*: *wisdom, prudence, trickery*. For them, *mètis* is used when there is no obvious solution, no tried and true recipe, no best way, but rather where the discovery of each hidden issue requires the creation of a new solution, an innovative approach. And let's remember that Mahomet described war simply as "a series of actions designed to trick the enemy."

Because it derives from persuasion, the lateral approach has therefore been favored in many cultures. It has, however, been treated with suspicion in the Western world, thus adding to its ambiguity. This ambiguity is demonstrated very well by the French word *malin*, which characterizes not only the fox in the fable but also Dame Weasel and many other characters La Fontaine brought so well to life. The word *malin* comes from the Latin *malignus*,[8] and means both *mean/evil* and *sly/crafty*. Besides, there is a "gray area" between finesse and trickery. In a thesaurus, what would we find under the word *crafty*? Words as diverse as *subtle, artful, sharp*, which are in no way pejorative, but also *sly, tricky, cunning*, which most certainly are.

In the Europe of the Middle Ages, the code of knighthood recommended the frontal attack, and stratagems, which were associated with the behavior and methods of the devil, were anything if not suspect.[9] They are only found in popular literature like the *Roman de Renard*. It is true, though, that Louis XI was an exception. He owes his kingdom to the traps he constantly set for all his enemies, Charles the Bold in particular. A few years later, Nicolas Machiavelli renewed the antique tradition of using stratagems, but with additional emphasis. He made the psychological battle a resulting dimension of the art of war. Machiavelli however has always been viewed with caution. The adjective *Machiavellian* says it all.

Karpov – In Russian, we have the word *khitryi* which means *skillful, ingenious, hard to read, crafty.* But *khitryi* also means *unscrupulous, wily,* or *devious.* Combine all of these traits into one and you have a character that could be embodied by Nikita Krushchev.

And among the chess players, I think that the word *khitryi* could describe a player like Petrosian.

Kouatly – Is it a term you would apply to yourself?

Karpov – Me? No, I don't think so ... only under certain circumstances ...

Kouatly – Isn't a good negotiator more or less Machiavellian?

Phelizon – He would certainly be better served by Hermes—the god of language—than by Ares—the god of war. I mean that he must constantly be able to create stratagems. The essence of negotiation is acting with finesse. All negotiations are battles with specific rules. What are those rules? Obviously, honesty associated with respect for the other and what he says (you must create an atmosphere of trust with your counterpart); maintaining the dialogue at all costs (you must create channels for passing messages before the situation is blocked); and time management (you must spring your arguments at the right time to create the effect of surprise).

Kouatly – When you are short on means, or when you want to save your means, isn't creating a stratagem the best thing to do?

Phelizon – A stratagem is a hidden action designed to surprise the enemy; either he doesn't see it, or the seduction has made him myopic, or he even harbors illusions.

The purpose of this hidden action is clearly to lure, maneuver, or destabilize the other, by putting him in a position that he had not planned on assuming from the beginning. The soldier's maneuver when operating by surprise, the hunter's trap and ambush, the navigator's art in bringing his ship safely to port against winds and seas, the lawyer's skillful wordplay in using his counterpart's argument against him, the banker's or salesperson's resourcefulness as he speculates on the market, the politician's careful prudence in determining which way public opinion will go. Stratagems preside over all the activities where a person "must learn to manipulate hostile forces, too powerful to be directly controlled, but that can be used despite them, without ever confronting them head on, to achieve the planned result through an unforeseen path."[10]

Karpov – As I said previously, it is through the introduction of new variations that you create surprise in chess. But you don't come up with a variation every day. A good stratagem consists of revealing it at the perfect moment. That's what *khitryi* is all about: retaining your "secret thrust," as they say in fencing, until you need it.

Let's just suppose, for example, that you come up with an interesting idea. You've carefully prepared it during your training sessions. Some particularly impatient players will want to use it immediately. Others will prefer to wait. Or, more subtly, they will reveal it a little at a time, just to see how their opponent reacts. For at the beginning, your opponent pays close attention to everything you do. Then he gets used to your style. So, perhaps around the fourth or fifth game, it's a good time to throw in the variation. If you do it that way, he won't overreact. He won't sense the danger because you will have made him used to the fact that your novelties are relatively harmless. But this time, it's different. Your opponent is caught short; you have completely tricked him.

THE PSYCHOLOGICAL HANDICAP[11]
I think that basically Spassky lost this match for psychological reasons. I don't know why, but he seemed unsure of himself in his openings and also in the execution of the strategies he chose. I am convinced that in some games, Spassky lost confidence in his own ability, with the inevitable result that his fighting spirit was dulled. Psychological handicaps are sometimes enough to decide the outcome of a battle between two protagonists.

That's what I did with Seirawan[12] during a game played in the early 1980s. I wrote a detailed commentary about it in one of my books.[13] When I unveiled my variation, Seirawan didn't have a chance. He forfeited very quickly. I remember also a stratagem that I used during a match against Timman[14] in 1979 in Montreal. He saw his defense fall apart in a flash. I won easily. In both cases, I had "managed" the element of surprise.

In chess, that's what a stratagem is: a move that surprises the opponent and with which you hit him at the worst possible time, when his forces start to fade.

Kouatly – There is nothing immoral about using a stratagem?

Phelizon – Well, at least nothing *amoral*. For contrary to a direct approach, the use of a stratagem is not meant to destroy the opponent, but to blur his vision of future events, to create *chance* in his mind, in a word to "de-structure" him in order to better appropriate his forces and resources.

So, a stratagem aims at deflecting the opponent's vision at the conceptual stage, not at the execution stage. By tricking him instead of destroying him, the goal is to inhibit him, to deprive him of his ability to react, to paralyze him. Beware, though, tricking is not lying. It is more like displacing the issue, displacing the focus, or more specifically blinding the adversary by unveiling the peripheral in order to better hide the important.[15]

Let's listen to Liddell Hart analyze the extremely risky— but successful—landing of Wolfe against the French rear forces above Quebec: "*Baiting* the enemy to draw him out of his reinforced position was not enough; he had to be led and dragged far from there. Another lesson was learned by the unsuccessful feints he used to try to prepare his direct action: *mystifying* the enemy was not enough, the enemy also had to be *distracted*, this term implying that his intelligence needed to be fooled by a diversion, and that simultaneously his freedom of movement needed to be sufficiently implicated that it would be impossible for him to respond with all his forces being spread out."[16] Baiting, mystifying, distracting: these are the essential elements of a stratagem.

Kouatly – Are you also saying that the best way to neutralize the enemy is to affect his morale?

THE ART OF CALCULATING PROBABILITIES[17]

A ruse is tricking someone into thinking you are there when you are not, that you have this or that plan when you don't—and with such probability that to face an imaginary danger, the opponent (whose forces are obviously limited) takes precautions that weaken him elsewhere, especially where you plan on striking. A ruse is the ability to make the enemy change his calculation of the probabilities.

Phelizon – War comes to an end usually when one of the camps *believes* they've lost. As Tang Zhen states so well, "He who knows how to sow confusion among the enemy, reaps the victory."[18] So, it is not enough to concentrate your forces, surprise the enemy, and attack him at the perfect spot, you must also break his spirit to deliver the decisive blow.

As long as his spirit is not broken, as long as the opponent does not admit defeat, nothing is decided. The reed of the fable withstands the storm because it is flexible.

Against the imposing army of Napoleon, Alexander I was victorious in the end because he refused to admit he was beaten. When attempting to paralyze your enemy, you must therefore determine his breaking point, *where he will go too far*. It is because he is convinced that engaging or pursuing the conflict is pointless that the enemy finally surrenders and accepts the terms you seek to impose. In a famous book, Stefan Zweig gave a very good description of the precise moment when the enemy's resolve begins to teeter. That's when the battle reaches what von Clausewitz called the *Kulminations Punkt*, that point when the attacker's forces are barely enough to keep him on the defensive while waiting for the opponent to unleash his counterattack.

WHEN CZENTOVIC NO LONGER UNDERSTANDS[19]

But, before looking away, something new and unexpected happened, Czentovic looked up and examined our ranks. He was obviously trying to figure out who was suddenly resisting with such energy. From that point on, our excitement was unleashed. If up until then we had no hope, the idea of breaking Czentovic's cold arrogance now made our adrenaline pump. Our new friend had already decided on the next move. My fingers were trembling when I grabbed the spoon to knock on the glass.

It was at that moment that we savored our first victory. The champion, who had always played standing up, hesitated, and then finally sat down. With regret he let himself fall heavily into his seat: no mind, he no longer showed his superiority by dominating physically over us. We forced him to get on the same level as us, at least spatially. He thought for a few moments, bent over the chessboard, so that we could barely see his eyes, under dark lids. . . .

Kouatly – Words that correspond to strength moves are directive and primary. What type of words are used for the lateral approach?

Phelizon – To influence morale strength, the language must be metaphorical, using words that speak to the imagination. It's the language that conjures up images, the language of parables and promises. Unlike words that incite, these words have broad meaning and little depth.

Why is a metaphor convincing? Because far from specifying the future in great detail to make it predictable, which characterizes direction and prescription, it targets emotions. Like Bonaparte telling the soldiers of the Italian army that the "plains of the Pô river are the most fertile in the world,"[20] or the new owner of a business in trouble, when he tells his employees that their "situation will improve considerably" after the restructuring efforts that he is asking them to accept. The same is true of many political leaders who have no qualms about promising their supporters "happy days ahead." Since the human heart is only sensitive to pictures—"a picture is worth a thousand words," says an old Eastern proverb—metaphorical language is the only one that registers and is therefore by its very nature *believable*. This is the language a strategist must adopt when he wants the other to listen to him (or when he sets out to seduce him). And it's through metaphor that he can reinforce the morale of his own troops and destroy those of the enemy.

Kouatly – Anatoly, how do you see the lateral approach in chess?

Karpov – To answer your question, I will tell you a personal story. I happened to be pretty close to Korchnoi and his family, because for four years we both lived in Leningrad. I even had a chance to secretly help him prepare for the qualifying match for the world championships. Why secretly? Because, at that time, Korchnoi was the *leader* of the Trade Unions team and I was playing for the Red

Army team. Korchnoi was supposed to play the qualifying match against Geller, the *leader* of the Red Army team. My trainer who was also Geller's trainer was very close to Korchnoi. He told me that we could absolutely not help Korchnoi, but that I, on the other hand, could help him train, on the condition that it remain a secret. So, I had played quite a bit with Korchnoi and thus got to know him very well. I knew that he never left anything to chance and was the kind of perfectionist who wanted to be fully trained, feel in perfect health, be confident that he had all the energy he needed, and demanded that all of the conditions of the match be set by him.

A short time after, in 1974, I had to play an official match against Korchnoi. We disagreed on where the match should take place. I didn't really care, but I knew it was an important issue to him. Korchnoi wanted to play in Leningrad, or in a Baltic region city, Riga or Talinn. I wasn't too keen on Leningrad, since that's where Korchnoi was born, had a lot of friends, and was much better known than I. It must be said also that our living conditions were a lot different in those days. Korchnoi lived in a large apartment and I still didn't have a place of my own.

Kouatly – So, what were the cities that you finally chose?

Karpov – I offered Moscow or any city in the south of the Soviet Union. The authorities realized that this match was important since the winner would play Fischer. Moscow was interested and was heard from, through the intermediary of the Minister of Sports and the Moscow Chess Federation. But Korchnoi was immovable. After conceding a few points in my favor, he told me: "In exchange for all my concessions, go to Moscow and tell the minister you are okay with playing in Leningrad."

And that's what I did. I met the minister on a Tuesday morning at 9:30 and told him that we had agreed on the conditions for the match, including time and location: Leningrad. The minister replied that he accepted all the proposals except for the location. "We understood that the match would take place in Moscow. It has been a while since a major competition was held in Moscow. That's the main reason we would like it there." I told him that my agreement with Korchnoi was a package deal. He had conceded the start time, which was very important to me, but that in exchange I had to give him Leningrad even though I preferred Moscow.

When I got back to my hotel, Korchnoi called me. He said that he knew that I had met with the minister. I told him that I had submitted our agreement to him, including time and location. That's when he said to me, "You know, I've thought about it and I don't want to play at 5:00 in the afternoon as we had agreed. I want to start the match at 2:00."

Kouatly – So, he was putting the agreement back on the table.

Karpov – Absolutely. I repeated to him, just as I had told the minister three hours earlier that our agreement was a package deal and that if he changed the time, I would change the location. "That's your right," was his answer. And we started to argue.

I went back to the Minister of Sports and immediately requested an urgent meeting. "What is it?" asked the minister, surprised. I recounted my telephone conversation with Korchnoi and told him that as long as the start time for the match was kept at 5:00 PM, the location wasn't that important.

Kouatly – And was it Moscow?

Karpov – His response was that he would be very happy to organize the match in Moscow and that of course, it would start at 5:00 PM and that everything else would be as we had agreed upon originally. That's the match where I noticed the psychologist on my opponent's team and decided to add one to mine.

In this episode, I let someone else decide an issue that was important to my opponent. The end of the story is well known: I won the match and became the world champion the following year after Fischer defected.

Kouatly – Let's talk now about the ins and outs of the lateral approach. Jean-François, I suppose this is the approach that is the most used in the business world.

Phelizon – The lateral approach is very popular in the economic world. After all, what is establishing a clientele if not making potential buyers get used to consumer behavior that presents obvious advantages to the seller?

You could almost say that everything in business is a stratagem. Here are a few very commonly used marketing stratagems:

- The Brand Loyalty Stratagem—the goal of which is to create familiarity, tie a specific consumer to a specific brand. It comes from the evidence that repetition is often enough to convince.
- The Detergent Stratagem—the goal here is to attract customers by offering something new, selling the same product under different names or in different packages. For example, selling the same detergent with different additives, and therefore different prices.
- The Airline Stratagem—which targets a weak spot. First you segment the market, then you exploit strong demand in a closed segment, and therefore a need. For example, plane tickets bought at the last minute for a peak time are sold at the highest price.
- The Drugstore Strategem—which consists of grouping an offer including "good" and "bad" products, or selling a common product expensively because you value a service that comes with it, for example, by extending store hours.
- The Imitation Stratagem—which consists of closely analyzing the competition (new products and new services) and putting out similar products shortly after them. More colloquially, it's "riding the competition's coattails" in all his innovations.

Here are a few more, often used at the negotiating table:

- The Friendship Stratagem—which consists of smothering your counterpart with all kinds of considerate attentions to better attack him after. In a sense it amounts to strengthening the relationship to hide the competition.
- The Star System Stratagem—which consists of intimidating the other, and sometimes even threatening him. The star takes up the entire stage and doesn't hesitate to flaunt his mood swings. By impressing the others he hopes to get what he wants.
- The Detour Stratagem—which consists of allying yourself with a friend of the other party. As I mentioned before, you make all kinds of friendly overtures to the opponent's lawyer or banker so that, if needed, he can be a friendly messenger.

- The Hostage Stratagem—this is a very old stratagem. In ancient times, it consisted of kidnapping your enemy's most beautiful slave to provoke negotiations. Nowadays, you need only buy a bunch of company shares or entice a few key executives away before advising the Board that you're ready to negotiate.

Karpov – I think that all these stratagems, some of which are very *khitryi*, can be applied to many other situations than those found in the business world, and especially in chess.

Kouatly – More generally—what are the main ways to run a negotiation?

Phelizon – When using the lateral approach, there are three main ways to handle a negotiation. The first is the one used by Talleyrand.[21] It consists of getting the other party to accept a principle and then having him draw all the consequences with you. The second one is the one used by Kissinger.[22] It amounts to determining the points of antagonism and then to bring them closer, degree by degree, until an agreement is reached. Finally, the third is the one used by Gromyko,[23] where you start by demonstrating to the opponent that the problem to be addressed is *his* problem, and then convince him that you are willing to resolve it.

Kouatly – Other than stratagems, are there principles applicable to all negotiations?

Phelizon – There are many authors who have offered suggestions. Here is a sample of current thinking:

- When your opponent wants to attack, think instead about negotiating. When he tries to negotiate, go on the attack.
- Try to draw him off his position and surprise him with unusual arguments. That is the best way to discover his intentions.
- If you have the advantage and your opponent is tired, pressure him to conclude without giving him time to regroup.
- Always be ready to negotiate but never negotiate without being ready.

- Remember that even if an agreement needs to be reached in public, it must always be negotiated in secret.
- Never unilaterally give away something you could use as a bargaining chip.
- Never let your adversary underestimate your response to a threat.
- Never announce beforehand what you will not do.
- Always give your opponent a way to retreat without losing face.[24]

I think these principles are pertinent. I would like to stress, however, the one I find the most important and that is *never announce beforehand what you will not do.*

Kouatly – How can you guarantee a negotiation will remain secret when, sometimes, dozens of people know about it?

Phelizon – You must be extremely clear, and sometimes even brutal with the back-office teams. I recall that during one of the acquisitions of a publicly held company, we made everyone who knew of our discussions, even those only remotely aware, such as lawyers, bankers, employees both hourly and nonsalaried, sign a letter reminding them of their nondisclosure obligations and specifying that we would hold them personally and *legally* responsible in the event of a "leak." Result: nothing appeared in the press before the official announcement.

Kouatly – In a chess game, just as in negotiation sessions, it seems that you go through pressure periods where everything is at stake, and more relaxed periods where you observe each other.

Karpov – During those difficult times where everything is at stake, you must be very mindful of the signals that you unconsciously project and the words you choose. Gestures sometimes betray optimism, contentment, doubt, or fatigue. These are signs that a seasoned adversary can exploit.

Phelizon – More generally, all negotiators know these "innings" that indicate the alternating phases of construction and destruction. Sometimes a negotiator has to be constructive, look for a compromise, try to resolve an issue by being flexible. Sometimes he has to be destructive, refuse a compromise, minimize the opponent's overtures and make him expose himself. All negotiations are led with a savvy dose of these two contradictory attitudes that aim at putting your opponent off balance.

Executive strategy books tell you not to play the game by your competitor's rules. Surprise him by changing the rules. "If you are constantly being surprised by your enemy, the signal is clear: you have a defensive strategy, you're reacting. You must change. A proactive strategy is one that constantly takes the enemy by surprise and puts him on the defensive."[25]

Kouatly – Does a chess player need to have a sense of compromise?

Karpov – No, I don't think it has a place in a chess match.

Kouatly – Sometimes, a simple turnaround is enough to surprise your adversary or escape a dangerous situation.

Phelizon – Of course. I once had to negotiate the sale of a major business branch in my company. The opposing team was difficult and discussions ran practically *nonstop* for a good twenty days. One evening, the discussion covered the accounting for *leasings* in the consolidated balance sheet. After a certain threshold, these were normally considered debts: but the threshold hadn't been determined during the preceding sessions.

So, I announced that some *leasings* didn't appear on the balance sheet, emphasizing that the rents attached to these *leasings* were recorded in the results. My counterpart did not take this well. He started by saying that he was quite surprised by this announcement, then gradually started to get angrier until finally he shouted that all of this was a "disgrace." He was angry and made a move to get up. I could have let him, but I would have put myself in a weak position and run the risk of being forced to have to concede another point. Instead, as cool as a cucumber, I said, "I'm not sure the word 'disgrace' really applies to this situation, or perhaps I don't understand all the subtleties of the English language." Everyone at the table burst out laughing and the issue of *leasings* was dropped.

Kouatly – Chinese authors could say that the art of negotiation consists of transforming the "fulls" into "empties" and vice versa.

Phelizon – Yes, that's another way of looking at the lateral approach. We said before that it is more economical than the other two approaches. It is also the one that gives you the most freedom of action. This is where the notions of "fulls" and "empties" come in. For there are approximately two ways to disrupt your opponent's analysis: dissuasion and suggestion. Dissuasion aims at decreasing your adversary's determination, therefore "emptying the full" by destroying his morale. Conversely, suggestion aims at creating illusion by suggesting dangers to your opponent where they don't really exist, therefore "filling his voids" and making him worry.

Kouatly – When playing chess, you always try to plan a few moves ahead. How does a player know that his analysis is more thorough than his opponent's?

Karpov – He can never be sure. For the mind doesn't work like a computer.

Actually, everything begins with the match preparation. That's when you determine your potential strengths and weaknesses in relation to the player you face. That's how you determine your openings. After that, you go through an in-depth analysis of your opponent. What are his favorite moves? How does he react to something new? What are his personality flaws? Then you begin to design your attack plan, your strategy.

It's only after all this that you can actually begin the in-depth analysis. When you have decided how you will wage your battle, you should be prepared to anticipate your opponent's moves. You should be able to get into his head, play like him. So, actually, there are four parts: what you want to do, how your adversary will react, what you think he wants to do, and how you will react. In the final analysis it will be styles that you have to grasp.

When you are sitting across from a flesh and blood opponent, his game should be as familiar to you as possible. And that's how, and only how, you can *deepen* your analysis.

Kouatly – How long on average does the preparation you describe take?

Karpov – It is a lengthy and difficult job, and depends obviously on the player you are meeting. It usually takes me between four to twelve weeks of very intensive work.

Kouatly – To be able to anticipate a few moves ahead seems to me a consistent factor in any battle.

Phelizon – Yes, people in the military say that the best strategist is the one who is best prepared to anticipate a situation. If a stratagem manages to influence destiny, it is because it is firmly ahead of events. That's how it manages to thwart the opponent's moves almost as soon as he conceives them. Conversely, the worst way to wage war is to immobilize armies face to face, with no room to maneuver. Because losing the freedom to act results in the loss of initiative.

Kouatly – Some personalities are more prone to analysis, some are more intuitive. Do you find different playing styles from country to country? Do Latin players like Capablanca play differently from Anglo-Saxon players like Fischer or Kasparov?

Karpov – In chess, there are styles and approaches, but there are also national characteristics. In Russia, these last years, we've had very good players, but no exceptional players, which is a problem. In Germany and Japan, high-level players can master technique but they sometimes seem to have trouble when they find themselves in a new situation. This is not the case for the Russians. For centuries, we have always considered that laws were made to be broken. Perhaps, that is why we tend to be so creative.

I don't think that Kasparov has what could be called an Anglo-Saxon style. True, he is very analytical, but he can also be creative. His problem may be that he doesn't like to take risks because he is afraid to lose. If he faces a player for whose style he hasn't been able to get a feel, he can be so uncomfortable that he prefers to forfeit.

Kouatly – Can you say something about the national styles of Indian and Chinese players?

Karpov – The general consensus is that chess was invented in India. They had excellent players in the nineteenth century. There were many less in the twentieth century, I am not really sure why. Anand is an exception. He possesses prodigious memory and physical stamina. I think his weakness lies perhaps in preference for the lateral approach. Like many Indians, he does not seem to like direct confrontation. But lately I've noticed a change. He's become a little less *kyitryi*. . . .

For a long time, and still today, the Chinese have played a very interesting form of chess with two teams of sixteen pawns moving on a large board made up of nine by ten spaces with a "river" that separates both camps.[26] The Chinese therefore have really only been playing international chess for about thirty years and have only started participating in international competition since 1975–1976. Today's Chinese players are making rapid progress. One day they should be at the highest level of world competition.

Kouatly – There is a final moment that ends all battles and negotiations. What is the attitude of the parties at that moment?

Phelizon – The last session of a negotiation always has a very particular atmosphere. Both parties talk about deal breakers, but no one really believes it. Then it's up to the last issue in contention, sometimes bitterly disputed, as if they wanted the game to continue.

I remember the last session of a negotiation, where, after a number of weeks of discussion, everything was settled except the very final price. It was a Wednesday, and it was about 3:00 in the morning. Everyone wanted to get some rest after a series of exhausting "all-nighters." The sale price I was asking was 5,650 million francs, but I could go down to 5,600. The buyer had offered 5,600 but refused to go any higher. We had taken several breaks and everyone was dug into their position.

What should I do? Should I accept 5,600 or keep fighting? As we were coming back into the room after a break, I approached my counterpart and said in a confidential tone. "You say yes to 5,625 and I'll take you all to dinner after the closing." He looked at me for a moment and shook my hand. A few weeks later both teams went to dinner at one of the best restaurants in Paris. My bill was huge, but it was well worth the 25 million francs I managed to "nibble" at the last minute.

Kouatly – Listening to the both of you, I get the impression that the lateral approach gets your vote.

Karpov – It doesn't get all my votes, but it certainly shouldn't be ignored, far from it.

In order to become a chess player at the highest level, you must be capable of finding original, winning moves at the right time. What makes the difference between a good player and an exceptional player is his ability to vary his approach. Sometimes he'll barge ahead, sometimes he'll "play" with the strengths and weaknesses of his opponent, and other times he will be more subtle and employ a stratagem. For me, this diversity in approach is what constitutes the real strength of a player.

Phelizon – One of the advantages of the lateral approach is that it doesn't automatically lead to the destruction of the adversary, but rather, as I've said, to his "destructuring." By favoring the destruction of his morale over his physical strength, the strategist kills two birds with one stone. He doesn't content himself with impeding the enemy; he gets stronger at his detriment.

It is only too well known how efficient shadow combats can be over time when they are led with determination. It is undeniably true that no form of warfare exploits the weaknesses of an adversary like guerilla warfare.

A CONFUSING RULE[27]

Fighters in the brush create contingencies: that's the idea behind the ambush. Areas of groves, woods, brush, gorges, when occupied by a moving population, spontaneously apply this method of multiplying hazards far from any front or war zone. Regular troops consider that these guerillas are not playing by the rules, even though they follow with intelligence the laws of probability, which are the fundamental laws of any confrontation be it in a game, sales, debate, politics, or war.

The lateral approach is more subtle and less immediate than the direct approach, or even the indirect approach, because it presupposes that you can convince the opponent to stop fighting. Obviously, that is only possible by taking into account the time factor and all the psychological factors that could influence him.

But this third approach is more effective than the other two and is a better response to the principle of economizing your strength that Marshall Foch considered so important. That is the reason why it is often adopted when you dispose of forces that are considerably weaker than those of the opponent. In an open game, the balance of forces is irrelevant and, just like David slaying Goliath, it is possible for the weak to beat the strong. Furthermore, when using finesse, time can be an ally. The lateral approach plays precisely on the progressive whittling down, or attrition, of the enemy's strength.

That being said, I agree with Anatoly when he says that the lateral approach cannot get all the votes. First, it is difficult to implement since the protagonists are on an even level from the psychological standpoint. It is obviously easier to decide a war than to convince your adversary that it is in his best interest to negotiate a compromise. It also assumes excellent "intelligence," not only as to the moves of the opponent, but also as to his intentions and even his beliefs. To create an illusion for someone, you must get at the emotional level. Finally, and most importantly, the lateral approach does not guarantee a sure win. Nothing says that the opponent will let himself be convinced to throw in the towel. Even worse, he can himself create confusion by his own finesse moves.

A battle of stratagems can quickly become a combat where the clearest mind and the shrewdest intelligence prevail. In that sense, the winner of the combat is the one who can best exploit a paradoxical, disadvantageous, or even desperate situation.

The winner is the one who can best turn contradictions to his advantage.

Kouatly – You mean by modifying the rules if necessary?

Phelizon – Playing with finesse is managing to detour the other's will, and use not only his physical forces but also his mind, his goodwill, his own determination against him.

The lateral approach is essentially dissuasive or suggestive and amounts to making the adversary react, which in any event will make him vulnerable. For he will be forced to modify his strategy, his own game plan, or at least adopt a new game plan different from the one he originally devised.

CHAPTER 5

After Victory, Look Ahead

Digest victories and defeats, learn from them.
– Stay modest. – Extend thanks to the team. –
Keep motivation up. – Psychology can benefit
but not replace technique. – Learn substance,
form, and method. – Innovate. – Don't lose
sight of the objective. – Chess and business:
intellectual labyrinth.

After victory, tighten your helmet cord.
Japanese proverb

Kouatly – Let's take a look now at the situation after the battle. The winning team starts by celebrating its victory. What next?

Karpov – After the victory, life goes on!

I am myself a bit of an exception among chess players. Russians love to celebrate their victories. And they are not always very objective when they explain the reasons for their victories or failures. I'm not really sure why, but I have always been very different. I am not very Russian when it comes to that. Actually, I'm a little indifferent about winning, or losing; in any case I harbor no illusions either way. I think I just know how to remain very pragmatic.

If I win, I try to understand why. If I lose, I tell myself there will be other occasions to win in the future. I know that even if I won ninety matches out of a hundred that I play, I would still have lost ten. As soon as you begin the battle, you become somewhat philosophical and realize that you can't always win.

Also, all battles are not of equal importance. You must be able to distinguish which are of consequence and which are not.

Kouatly – But you do celebrate your victories a little.

Karpov – For a long time, I never organized a party at the end of a competition. I'm lucky in that I can regroup very quickly after a big effort. That's why I've been able to participate in so many tournaments in my life while staying at the head of the group of world-class players. After completing a tournament, I can go right on to the next one almost without stopping. Spassky once said that every time he competed in a world championship, he lost a year of his life. That's not how it's been for me. Even after the most difficult fights that I've had to wage during my thirty-year career, I've always been able to get back to work within two or three weeks. Often, someone will congratulate me on a recent victory that I'd almost forgotten about because I was already engaged in a new battle.

I think that you can't spend your life rehashing your victories, or your defeats. You must learn to digest them and forget them. I've long believed that a victory might be good for your image and reputation, but won't help insure your future career. So, as they say, "After a victory, it is time to tighten your helmet."[1]

Phelizon – La Fontaine also wrote, "An insolent victor works towards his defeat."[2]After a confrontation, clearly both parties need to remain realistic. And what does that mean? It means that a battle is at best just one of the episodes that mark a history. So, for the losing camp, it is a time to regroup. And for the winning camp, it is a time to think about what comes next. Losing a battle is not the end of a story, and neither is winning. There will always be other challenges.

Achieve and *win* are verbs that must be used with an object. You cannot use "achieve" all by itself, nor "win" all by itself. You only achieve a milestone in a career, and win within the framework of a strategy. You must therefore know how to exploit a victory or a defeat. Let's remember Maharbal's famous, foreshadowing reply to Hannibal after the battle at Cannes: "The Gods did not give everything to the same man. Hannibal, you know how to win, but not profit from your victory."[3]

THE BATTLE OF CANNES[4]

The next morning, Varron led his troops out of the camp and offered to fight; it was just the battle Hannibal was hoping for. As was the custom for both parties, the infantry was placed in the center and the cavalry on the wings, but Hannibal's lineup, considered closely, was unusual; he advanced the Gauls and the Spaniards who formed the center of the infantry line, whereas he kept his elite African soldiers at the rear, placed at each end of the line. The Gauls and the Spaniards created a sort of natural magnet attracting the Roman infantry, and as anticipated, they were overrun, so that the Carthaginian line which had been approximately convex turned concave.

Encouraged by this apparent first success, the Roman legionnaires crowded into the breach; the backup grew denser and denser to the point where the Romans could barely wield their weapons. And, even though they thought they had already caved in the Carthaginian front, they were actually advancing deeper and deeper into the enemy mass. At that moment, Hannibal's veteran African troops converged on the center from the two wings, a move that automatically resulted in enveloping the Romans on each other.

This maneuver created a situation and a trap similar to the one experienced at sea at Salamine; but at Cannes this maneuver was better prepared and calculated. This move could be called "the tactic of collective *jiû-jitsu*," *jiû-jitsu* being essentially based on the indirect approach.

During this time, on the left wing, Hannibal's heavy cavalry shredded the enemy cavalry; then sweeping everything on the Roman rear guard, it scattered the other wing's cavalry which had been contained by the light Numidian cavalry, particularly well suited to skirmishes. The pursuit having been entrusted to the Numidians, the heavy cavalry dealt the final blow by charging onto the rear of the Roman infantry. Already surrounded on three sides and too crowded, they offered no resistance at all.

At that point, the battle degenerated into a massacre: by Polybe's account, of the 76,000 men in the Roman army, 70,000 fell, among them Paul-Émile. Varron was able to escape unharmed from the disaster for which he was responsible.

Kouatly – So, in essence, you both advise the winner to stay modest and the loser to look up.

Karpov – Yes, in all instances, it is best to forget the battle and get right back to hard work.

But this doesn't just apply to chess or business. I would make the same recommendation to a soldier, an athlete, a politician, or a movie star.

Rather than bask in success, it is certainly better as Jean-François said *to be humble to the experience.*

Kouatly – Are there often debriefing sessions after a winning negotiation or a chess match?

Phelizon – In a large company, negotiations come one after the other. Some go well, others not so well, and still others fail. After a successful operation, I agree with Anatoly that showy events should be avoided and that press releases issued by both sides at the conclusion of a deal should always be accurate and succinct.

I also think that the team leader should assemble his team and start by thanking everyone for their hard work. The back-office often gives their all, if only by working long hours, and I think that should be recognized. Next, he should go over the sequence of discussions with their high points and the reasons for a decision having gone one way or the other. The members of his team can then tell him what they did or tried to do and discuss the difficulties they encountered and how they could improve.

But, don't get me wrong. While the debriefing session is important, it's not as much to "give back to Caesar" as to keep the team motivated and willing to perform the next time. Selecting and motivating a team *before*, making few changes *during*, keeping it together *after*, this is what I think the general attitude should be.

Karpov – After a match, of course I am happy to go have a drink with my team and thank them for their help. But when everything has gone well, I don't conduct a debriefing with my colleagues. I reserve the postmortems for the times when we have not done well. Then we analyze every move in detail and draw conclusions for the future.

Kouatly – Does the team psychologist participate in this meeting?

Karpov – No, these meetings are technical and would be of no interest to the psychologist. I usually see him one on one, very little before or after a competition; mostly between matches.

Kouatly – So, if the psychologist doesn't participate in the match preparation, his role is mainly tactical.

Karpov – In the chess world there are different kinds of competition. There are matches, tournaments, and games. In my life, I have participated in more than 200 matches, eleven of which were world championships, and countless tournaments. For quite a while I have been convinced that psychology plays a major part in matches. It's different for a tournament. You meet many different players and everything is more technical, even if from time to time you can use some stratagems, especially for opening moves. But, in a match, especially at the highest levels of world championships, psychological aspects are crucial and can determine the outcome of the confrontation.

You must therefore take into account these psychological aspects when you are creating the general strategy you will deploy in your game plan. And you must view them differently for every game you play. What I mean by this is that there is a strategic psychology and a tactical psychology. The first applies to the positional game. It helps you determine the general framework for your action. The second applies to the combination game. It helps you continue to play, and especially keep the advantage. In order to combine all these psychological aspects at each stage of the match, you must not only establish a "psychological profile" of the opponent, but also determine that of all those who assist him. By knowing what the opponent's advisor might recommend to his boss, you will be in a better position to understand the ins and outs of the battle you are waging.

Kouatly – Simply put, which is better: excellent psychological analysis and average technique, or average psychological analysis and excellent technique?

Karpov – There are many works of fiction in Russian literature. One of them tells the story of a very creative and *khitryi* man who wanted to be a millionaire. He arrived one day in a small village in Oural and introduced himself to the local chess club as a grand master from Moscow. Despite the fact that he barely knew how to move the pawns on the board, he made an offer to the president of the club to give a class to the best players in town before participating in an exhibition match with them. The class was a great success because the man was an excellent speaker. For two hours he showed his captivated audience that if Peter is a good chess player and Paul a bad one, nothing will make Paul win. The exhibition match on the other hand was not such a success.

All of this is to demonstrate that psychology can be a great benefit to technique but certainly not replace it.

During a famous match in Moscow, Capablanca played opposite a much weaker but very cunning player. During one whole game, this player made Capablanca think that the best he was hoping for was a draw. When Capablanca suddenly realized this opponent was actually on the verge of beating him, it was too late. He lost the match—and confounded the odds.

Phelizon – In the business world, I don't think that is the way it works. If you have excellent psychology and average technique, you can easily get rich. But if you have average psychology and excellent technique, it's a good bet that you'll be doing the same job for the rest of your life.

Kouatly – Jean-François, what advice would you give a beginner about to jump into a negotiation?

Phelizon – I would make the distinction between substance, form, and method. When it comes to substance, I would tell him that credibility is a success factor that must be cultivated. You can easily lose credibility by making promises that you won't keep or threats that you won't enforce. But it can also be harmed by unrealistic proposals, especially for price or service.

As to form, I would insist that any dollar issue can be negotiated. You have to learn to be displeased with a number, regardless of the amount, and systematically ask if the other party can do better. What should constantly be going through your mind is, "This is all well and good, but can you make another effort?"

Finally, when it comes to method, I suggest keeping two lists: one for the issues both parties agree on and cannot be renegotiated, and the other for the items in contention. Discussions should concentrate on exchanging points for others on the second list, with each partial agreement completing the first list.

So, to sum up, it seems to me that in order to efficiently lead a successful negotiation, you must concentrate on form as much as substance, the way to lead discussions as much as the object of the deal.

Kouatly – How about you Anatoly? What are the two or three pieces of advice you would like to pass on to a young hopeful?

Karpov – What I would tell him is that you have to work hard and do everything possible to be innovative. It is very important to develop your own ideas. That is the best way to develop self-confidence.

I can't remember how many new moves I came up with during my thirty-year career. I always have one or two in reserve. There was one that I had conceived for a specific opponent and that I kept to myself for a long time, at least eight years.

So, study and innovate, but also fight. Study continuously as if time was counted and always fight as if victory were unattainable.

♟

STUDY AND FIGHT[5]

If you are trying to learn to play chess through books, you will soon discover that only the opening and ending moves can give a complete schematic description of this game. The game's immense complexity right after that beginning defies all description. It is only by seriously studying the way the masters play that you can fill the holes in your knowledge.

Kouatly – More generally, it is possible to conceive of tactics that are not at the service of strategy?

Phelizon – Strategy in the sense that I understand it should be the *ultimate concern* of the one in charge. His job should be to constantly review and assess, leading him to establish and refine his vision of the future. This vision appears both improbable at the beginning and necessary after the fact, but it will however become his destiny. He will not stop putting it into the perspective of a strategic action.

Let's take the example of a business that wants to grow in the distribution sector: that's the president's vision. Putting this vision in perspective might include the acquisition of a number of businesses within the sector. But a specific acquisition will only be one episode in the life of this business. That is how Compagnie de Saint-Gobain acquired first Poliet and Lapeyre in France, then Meyer in Great Britain, and finally Raab Karcher in Germany. These three "battles" were led within a specific strategy: to make this group the European leader in Building Products Distribution.

It has been my opinion for a while now that strategy should be assimilated to a direction, a path taken together. The Chinese character *dào* synthesizes the meaning of strategy in that sense.[6] *Dào* means road, path, doctrine—and by extension to lead or teach. And what is strategic action if not advancing a group within the framework of a "doctrine" meaning an action plan?

So, it is in light of the *dào* that one must understand what a battle is. It is a collective action undertaken within the framework of a given strategy. The consequence of all this is that you must never lose sight of the object you pursue. Your opponent might try to lead you astray, use rhetorical wizardry, or try to seduce you. In short, make a lot of useless noise. No matter. This should not detract you from the objective you set for yourself and that you must constantly consult, like a compass.

Kouatly – Some directions are more respectable than others. Should any kind of moral connotation be assigned to strategic action? Of the three approaches we discussed together, is there one that you find more "moral" than the others?

Phelizon – I am tempted to say that *in the heat of action, morality is silent.* By this however, I don't mean that a CEO can disregard ethical behavior, quite the contrary. Nor can he consider using immoral means to win. I only mean that when engaged in a battle, you are *ipso facto* on ground that is not that of morality.

It would be a mistake to favor one approach over another under the pretext that it is more "ethical." Who is to say that in a given context it is more ethical to destroy your enemy (direct action), use his strength without him knowing (indirect action), or lead him astray (lateral action)?

It is true that the natural human tendency is to use force. The direct approach is at the same time more instinctive and more "brilliant" than the others. Conversely, wisdom leads you more likely to adopt a lateral approach, at least in the beginning. It is harder to implement, but much more economical in means. This is how war can be considered the last solution.

Kouatly – Whatever the approach used to wage a battle, it would seem that the psychological components play a deciding part.

Karpov – Yes, I truly believe that and I hope that this little book has been able to convince the reader that once the strategy is defined and the game plan established, the high-level player must also show a sense of finesse if he truly wants to win.

Phelizon – The three approaches that we have analyzed together as-sume to varying degrees that you have a good knowledge of your opponent. Therefore they cannot be chosen in a void.

Every action, even lateral, has a response. For example, antic-ipation might be enough to prevent your opponent from pursuing his objective and completely negate his preparations; dependency might keep him from accumulating resources or objections to use in his action or his rhetoric; division can disturb his movements as he tries to concentrate his forces; avoidance can reduce his freedom of movement and even perhaps dissuade him from attacking; delays might in some instances foil the effect of surprise. In my opinion, all of these parries, executed at the correct moment, are a show of finesse. It is not enough for them to be used at the appropriate time. They must also be adapted to the physical and mental state of the opponent.

Karpov – An image that comes to my mind, linking chess, negotiations, and business in general, is that of the labyrinth. Chess resembles an intellectual labyrinth in the sense that every time you open a door you find yourself faced with ten new doors that open onto the unknown. What playing chess teaches you is that you don't really have to know what you should do, but you do have to know what you should absolutely not do. That is how instinctively you will avoid some of the doors in the labyrinth.

Negotiations or business in general is also like a labyrinth. Every opened door gives way to more doors, every opportunity gives way to new opportunities. And just like chess, it is more important to determine with precision the opportunities you are not interested in than those you are. If I could paraphrase the Nixon precept that Jean-François cited earlier, "Always know ahead of time what you don't want." It isn't that easy and here again, only experience can whisper which roads you should not take.

I think that these five conversations have amply demonstrated that to have the best chance of winning, you must not only be well prepared, well informed, and well versed in the tactical aspects of combat, but you must also include the psychological profile of your opponent in the battle plan, or the exchange. For only a sense of finesse can assure the time and means management, without which a victory or an agreement could only be the result of chance.

APPENDIX

World Chess Champions Recognized by the World Chess Federation*

1	Wilhelm Steinitz	1886–1894
2	Emanuel Lasker	1894–1921
3	Jose-Raul Capablanca	1921–1927
4	Alexandre Alekhine	1927–1935
5	Machgielis (Maz) Euwe	1935–1937
	Alexandre Alekhine	1937–1945
6	Mikhaïl Botvinnik	1948–1957
7	Vasily Smyslov	1957–1958
	Mikhaïl Botvinnik	1958–1960
8	Mikhaïl Tal	1960–1961
	Mikhaïl Botvinnik	1961–1963
9	Tigran Petrosian	1963–1969
10	Boris Spassky	1969–1972
11	Robert James (Bobby) Fischer	1972–1975
12	Anatoly Karpov	1975–1985
13	Garry Kasparov	1985–1993
	Anatoly Karpov	1993–1999
14	Alexander Khalifman	1999–2000
15	Viswanathan (Vishy) Anand	2000–2002
16	Ruslan Ponomariov	2002–

*For more details, please consult the World Chess Federation Web site at www.fide.com.

Notes

PROLOGUE: ESTABLISH AND MAINTAIN A WINNING POSITION

1. José Raul Capablanca (1888–1942) was world champion from 1921 to 1927.

2. Gosplan, abbreviation of Gossoudarstvennyï Planovyïkomitet: Soviet department created in 1921 to create five-year economic development plans and administer their execution.

3. Mikhail Moiseyevich Botvinnik (1911–1995) was the U.S.S.R. champion seven times from 1931 to 1952, and world champion from 1948 to 1957, 1958 to 1960, and 1961 to 1963.

4. Boris Vasilievich Spassky (born in 1937) was world champion from 1969 to 1972, the year in which he relinquished the title to Bobby Fischer in a widely publicized match.

5. Viktor Lvovich Korchnoi (born in 1931) was international grand master in 1956. Despite never having won the world championship, he is often considered one of the greatest players of the twentieth century.

6. Sun Tzu, ca. 500 B.C., famous Chinese general; Karl von Clausewitz, 1780–1831, Prussian general and military strategist; Ferdinand Foch, 1851–1929, French military leader and Allied Supreme Commander during WW1; Basil Liddell Hart, 1895–1970, British military historian and strategist.

7. 722–481 B.C.

8. The Japanese have a particular way of conducting meetings. Decisions are often the object of a consensus established ahead of time by the protagonists, even before a formal decision meeting has been set.

This practice, called *nemawashi* (prior discussion), is designed to give the main participants time to smooth over their differences.

9. The first ten moves of a match can be played in about 1.6 quadrillion ways.

10. Stephan Zweig, *The Chess Player*, Le Livre de Poche, 1991, pp. 22–23.

11. François-André Danican Philidor (1726–1795) was a musical prodigy and the best player of his time. At twenty-two, he published *Analysis of the Game of Chess*, which has remained a classic.

CHAPTER 1: PREPARING FOR BATTLE

1. A. Karpov, *Chess, Learning and Progressing*, Economica, 1993, p. 97.
2. La Fontaine, *Fables*, I, 17.
3. See J.C. Humes, *Nixon's Ten Commandments of Leadership and Negotiation*, Touchstone, 1997, pp. 43–44.
4. Robert "Bobby" James Fischer (born in 1943) was the U.S. champion at fourteen, and the world champion from 1972 to 1975, when he relinquished the title to Karpov for refusing to play under the rules of the WCF (World Chess Federation), organizer of the world championships.
5. F. Walder, *Saint-Germain or Negotiating*, Gallimard, 1958, pp. 39–40.
6. Kliment Iefremovitch Vorochilov (1881–1969), politician and marshal of the Soviet army, commanded the Northwest front of the Red Army during World War II.
7. *Zheng*: balanced, normal, regular; *qi*: extraordinary, indirect, special.
8. Cf. J.-F. Phelizon, *Rereading the Art of War by Sun Tzu*, Economica, 1999, V 10–11. This translation of the *Art of War* will be used herein.
9. F. Walder, op. cit., p. 19.
10. Voltaire, *Zadig, or The Destiny, XIX*. French writer, satirist, and philosopher, Voltaire is remembered as a crusader against tyranny and bigotry. He treated the problem of evil in his classic tale *Zadig* (1747), which obliged him to go into exile in Potsdam, on the invitation of Frederic II of Prussia, then in Geneva.
11. Cf. J.-F. Phelizon, *Thirty Six Stratagems*, Economica, 2001, pp. 117–120.

CHAPTER 2: SELECT A STYLE AND APPROACH

1. Garry Kimovich Kasparov (born in 1963) took the world champion title from Karpov in 1985, but gave it back to him in 1993. Following differences with the World Chess Federation, Kasparov created his own organization: the PCA (Professional Chess Association), which twice

organized its own match for the world champion title: in 1993 (Kasparov–Short) and in 1995 (Kasparov–Anand). In 2003, Kasparov still held the title from the PCA.

2. Tigran Vartanovich Petrosian (1929–1984) became world champion in 1963 by beating Botvinnik. Spassky took the title from him in 1969.

3. "Resistant conciliation" is inspired by the *fourth stratagem*: "wait quietly while the enemy tires." Cf. J.-F. Phelizon, *Thirty Six Stratagems*, Economica, 2001, pp. 57–61.

4. La Fontaine, Fables, I, 8.

5. Mikhaïl Nekhemievich Tal (1936–1992) took the world championship title from Botvinnik in 1960, but he won it back in a grudge match in 1961.

6. Cf. J.-F. Phelizon, op. cit., pp. 73–76.

7. *Le Roman de Renard* (modern version by L. Chauveau), Payot, 1924, pp. 221–222.

8. J.C. Humes, *Nixon's Ten Commandments of Leadership and Negotiation*, Touchstone, 1997, p. 109.

9. "Hidden aggressiveness" is inspired by the *tenth stratagem:* "To hide a dagger in a smile." Cf. J.-F. Phelizon, op. cit., pp. 83–87.

10. Adapted from *Springs and Autumns*, chronicle attributed to Confucius (551–479 B.C.).

11. Viswanathan Anand (born in 1969) was the world champion from 2000 to 2002.

12. C.A. Sainte-Beuve, *Monday Talks (Causeries du Lundi)*, Garnier, S.d., t. I, p. 145.

13. Cf. B. Burrough and J. Helyar, *Barbarians at the Gate, the Fall of RJR Nabisco,* Jonathan Cape, 1990; or H. Lampert, *True Greed*, NAL Penguin, 1990.

14. See Sun Tzu, *The Art of War*, Vol. II, p. 5.

15. Napoléon, *Selected Texts (Textes Choisis)*, Plon, 1912, pp. 277–278.

CHAPTER 3: INDIRECT APPROACH: STRENGTH AGAINST STRENGTH

1. Tullus Hostilius, 672–641 B.C.

2. See Titus Livius, *History of Rome*, I, 25.

3. J.-F. Phelizon, *Thirty Six Stratagems*, Economica, 2001, p. 205.

4. Boris Spassky, *Fifty-One Annotated Games of the New World Champion*, FDR Books, 1969.

5. The term *bujutsu* covers all martial arts in feudal Japan. See O. Ratti and A. Westbrook, *Secrets of the Samurai: A Survey of Martial Arts of Feudal Japan*, C.E. Tuttle, 1973, p. 15.

6. Jigoro Kano (1860–1938) founded his judo school in 1882.

7. The Aïkido school was founded by Morihei Ueshiba (1883–1969).

8. See O. Ratti and A. Westbrook, op. cit., pp. 434 and 437.

9. The game of *Go* or *wei qi* in Chinese ("game of surrounding") was invented in China during the age of Springs and Autumns (722–481 B.C.). Useful information can be found in Ma Xiaochum, *The Thirty Six Stratagems Applied to Go,* Yutopian, 1996.

10. Sun Tzu masterfully demonstrated this opposition between emptiness (*xu*) and fullness (*shi*) in the sixth chapter of his book *The Art of War.*

11. See B.H. Liddell Hart, *World History of Strategy,* Plon, 1962, p. 375.

12. F. Jullien, *Detour and Access (Le D'etour et l'Accès),* Grasset, 1995, pp. 60–61.

13. Pierre Barthélemy, *Le Monde,* May 6, 1997.

14. Douglas R. Hofstadter, *Gödel, Esher, Bach: An Eternal Golden Braid,* Basic Books, 1999, p. 286.

CHAPTER 4: LATERAL APPROACH: PLAYING WITH FINESSE

1. See Sun Tzu, *The Art of War,* Vol. III, p. 2.

2. See Sun Tzu, *The Art of War,* Vol. IV, pp. 11–16.

3. See Phedrus, *Fables,* I, 13; *Le Roman de Renard (The Tale of Renard),* Payot, 1924, pp. 34–37; and of course La Fontaine, *Fables,* I, 2.

4. Alexander Alekhine (1892–1946), French player of Russian origin became world champion in 1927 by beating Capablanca. He lost his title in 1935 to Euwe, but took it back from him in 1937 and kept it until his death.

5. Sun Tzu, *The Art of War,* Vol. I, p. 18. See also Al-Muttaki, *Words Attributed to the Prophet (Paroles attribuées au Prophète),* in G. Chaliand, *World Anthology of Strategy (Anthologie mondiale de la Stratégie),* R. Laffont, 1990, p. 462.

6. La Fontaine, *Fables,* X, 4.

7. In Chinese, the character—(*jì*), calculation, plan, stratagem, is made up of two radicals, one of which means to *know how to pronounce,* or *count,* and the other, either *ten* (the decimal system number) or the *five cardinal points* (east, west, south, north, and center). By extension, *jì* means calculate, combine (see L. Weiger, *Chinese Characters,* Dover, 1965, p. 68).

8. *Malignus,* from the Latin word *malus* (bad, evil).

9. "That your words be: Yes? Yes! No? No! What you add comes from the Devil" (*Gospel according to St. Matthew,* V, 37).

10. M. Détienne and J.-P. Vernant, *Tricks of Intelligence (Les Ruses de l'Intelligence),* Flammarion, 1974, pp. 56–57.

11. Paul Keres, *Chess Life*, August 1974, referring to the eleventh game of the 1974 world championship semifinals between Karpov and Spassky.

12. Yasser Seirawan (born 1960) qualified twice for the world chess championships.

13. See Anatoly Karpov, *Anatoly Karpov's Best Games*, Chrysalis Books, 1996.

14. Jan Timman (born 1959) was the chess champion of the Netherlands eight times.

15. "To dupe is to take someone for a fool, tricking, and depriving at the same time. The word *dupe* comes from French slang: it's the same word as *huppe*, which is the name of a bird (lark). Since this bird had the reputation of not being very intelligent, crooks called their victims "dupes" (G. Gougenheim, *French Words in History and Everyday Life* (*Les Mots français dans l'histoire et dans la vie*), A. et J. Picard, 1966, t. I, p. 137).

16. B.H. Liddell Hart, *World History of Strategy* (*Histoire mondiale de la Strategie*), Plon, 1962, pp. 106–107; The English General James Wolfe (1727–1759) was mortally wounded at the battle of Abraham, a few days before the surrender of Quebec.

17. J. Guitton, *Thought and War* (*La Pensée et la Guerre*), Desclée de Brouwer, 1969, p. 156.

18. Tang Zhen, *Writings of an Unknown Sage* (*Ecrits d'un Sage encore inconnu*), Gallimard-Unesco, 1991, p. 320.

19. Stefan Zweig, *The Chess Player* (*Le joueur d'echecs*), Le Livre de Poche, 1991, pp. 38–39. Czentovic is supposed to be a worldwide chess champion in this famous novel.

20. Proclamation of March 27, 1796, Napoleon, *Selected Texts*, Plon, 1912, pp. 25–26.

21. Charles-Maurice de Talleyrand-Périgord (1754–1838) embraced the ideas of the Revolution in 1789 before becoming Minister of Exterior Relations under Napoleon I (until 1807) and then under Louis XVIII (in 1814 and starting in 1815).

22. Henry Alfred Kissinger (born 1923) was Secretary of State under the Nixon and Ford administrations from 1973 to 1977. He was the co-recipient of the Nobel Peace Prize in 1973 (along with Le Duc Tho, who refused it).

23. Andrei Andreyevich Gromyko (1909–1989) was the U.S.S.R. Foreign Minister from 1957 to 1985.

24. See R. Nixon, *The Real War* (*La Vraie Guerre*), A. Michel, 1980, p. 286.

25. M. Robert and M. Devaux, *Think Strategy* (*Penser Stratégie*), Dunod, 1994, p. 155.

26. Chinese chess (*xiáng qi*) is an adaptation of the Indian game *chaturanga* or the Persian game *shatrang*, which is the origin of the game

of chess as we know it today in the West. *Xiáng qi* or "the elephant game" symbolizes also war between two armies and victory is attained by mating the opposing king.

27. J. Guitton, *Thought and War (La Pensée et la Guerre)*, p. 158.

CHAPTER 5: AFTER VICTORY, LOOK AHEAD

1. Quoted by E. P. Hoyt, *Three Military Leaders*, Kodansha, 1933, p. 71.

2. La Fontaine, *Fables*, VII, 13.

3. Titus Livius, *Roman History (Histoire Romaine)*, XXII, 51. See also G. Walter, *The Destruction of Cartage (La Destruction de Carthage)*, Somogy, 1947, p. 347.

4. B.H. Liddell Hart, *World History of Strategy (Histoire Mondiale de la Strategie)*, Plon, 1962, pp. 35–36.

5. Sigmund Freud, "The Beginning of the Treatment," in *The Psycho-analytical Technique (Le début du Traitement, dans La Technique Psychanalytique)*, PUF, 1953, p. 80.

6. The character (*dào*) is made up of two radicals, one meaning *to go* and the other *forward* (see L. Wieger, *Chinese Characters*, Dover, 1965, p. 326).

About the Author

ANATOLY KARPOV, one of the greatest chess players of all time, became a chess master at age 15 and the world's youngest international
grand master in 1970. The winner of more than 130 international
chess tournaments and matches, he was World Champion from 1975
to 1985 and again from 1993 to 1999. He has written several books on
chess technique and strategy, including *Anatoly Karpov's Best Games*
and an autobiography, *Karpov on Karpov*, and is currently establishing
a network of chess schools around the world.

JEAN-FRANÇOIS PHELIZON is President and CEO of Saint-Gobain
Corporation, the holding company for the U.S.- and Canadian-based
business of the French multi-national corporation, Compagnie de
Saint-Gobain, one of the world's top 100 industrial companies. He
has published translations of Sun Tzu's *The Art of War* and *Thirty-Six
Strategems* and is the author of several books on business strategy and
management, including *Methods and Models for the Research Operation*
and *Strategic Action*, published by the leading French business and
economics publisher, Editions Economica.

BACHAR KOUATLY is an international grand master of chess and
editor of the magazine, *European Chess*.